Making Big Schools Feel Small

Multiage Grouping, Looping, and Schools-Within-a-School

Making Big Schools Feel Small

Multiage Grouping,
Looping,
and Schools-Within-a-School

Paul S. George
John H. Lounsbury

National Middle School Association
Westerville, Ohio

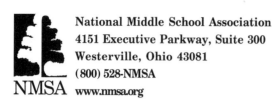

National Middle School Association
4151 Executive Parkway, Suite 300
Westerville, Ohio 43081
(800) 528-NMSA
NMSA   **www.nmsa.org**

Sue Swaim, Executive Director
Jeff Ward, Associate Executive Director
John Lounsbury, Senior Editor, Professional Publications
Edward Brazee, Associate Editor, Professional Publications
Mary Mitchell, Publications Editorial Assistant & Designer
Ruth Rauch, Publications Manager
Marcia Meade, Senior Publications Representative
Andrea Yost, Graphic Designer, cover design
Cheri Howman, Publications Assistant

Library of Congress Cataloging-in-Publication Data

George, Paul S.
    Making big schools feel small: multiage grouping, looping, and schools-within-a-school/Paul S. George, John H. Lounsbury,
    p. cm.
    Includes bibliographical references.
    ISBN 1-56090-165-9
    1. Middle schools--United States--Administration. 2. School improvement programs--United States. 3. Middle school teaching--United States.
    I. Lounsbury, John H. II. Title

LB1623.5.G45 2000
373.236--dc21   00-0055428

Contents

Acknowledgments

This publication, like all such studies, has drawn on the expertise and assistance of many individuals. We acknowledge with appreciation the contributions of the administrators, teachers, parents, and students who participated in the national survey.

In addition, many individuals made substantial contributions in various aspects of the study. Our thanks, therefore, go to Kathy Shewey, Margaret Heeney, Carol Smith, Jeanette Stern, Robert Lincoln, Mark Springer, Linda Hopping, Sue Kowalski, and Nancy Mizelle.

About the Authors

Paul S. George is Professor of Education in the Department of Educational Leadership at the University of Florida in Gainesville. For more than 30 years, Dr. George has been a leading advocate for middle level education in the United States and abroad. A much sought-after speaker and consultant, he has addressed over 80,000 people at various conferences, workshops, and universities. A prolific writer as well, he has authored hundreds of articles, monographs, and books, including *The Exemplary Middle School*, generally regarded as the standard text in the field.

John H. Lounsbury is Publications Editor for the National Middle School Association and Dean Emeritus, School of Education, Georgia College & State University, Milledgeville. A student of junior high school/middle school education for nearly 50 years, he is regarded as one of the founders of the middle school movement. Like Dr. George, he has spoken widely on behalf of young adolescents and published innumerable articles, research reports, and books, primarily dealing with middle school curriculum.

I
The Case for Smallness and
Long-Term Teacher-Student Relationships

Productive human groups of all kinds are, characteristically, stable and persistent. Healthy family life, profitable corporate efforts, winning sports teams, effective military operations, and successful religious organizations all depend, in part, on the quality, stability, and duration of the relationships among and between the members of the organization (Homans, 1950). Quality of life in family and peer groups is universally associated with long-term relationships, and, in recent years, business leaders have developed a lively interest in productive teams that cooperate closely over several years. Human productivity is tied, in important ways, to the quality and length of the human relationships at the heart of the effort (Ouchi, 1981; Peters & Waterman, 1982).

Even the military has capitalized on the benefits of long-term relationships achieved in small units. Using long-term relationships in small groups to make the organization as a whole more efficient, the American military has demonstrated the power of such groups on battlefields around the world. In fact, studies conducted on long-term relationships in the military show that when members of a small group are frequently removed and replaced, the group is less cohesive and efficient (Moskos, 1975). Similar evidence exists in other American institutions.

In education, by contrast, less value has recently been placed on long-term interpersonal relationships or size (Rosenholtz, 1989; Slavin, 1989). Contemporary learning groups in the American educational system at the middle and high school levels have a common design attribute – they only exist for a brief period. Homerooms, classes, teams, or other groups of teachers and students have a relatively short life-span and are, thus, characterized by brief and shallow teacher-student relationships. The basis for the organizational plan adopted is almost always focused exclusively on the curriculum of content, not the curriculum of climate.

In recent years, an increasing number of middle school educators have come to believe that the education of young adolescents can be enhanced in significant ways when teachers and students are members of classrooms and small team groups characterized by relationships that last for more than one period of the day and for longer than nine months. Long-term teacher-student relationships in middle schools, these educators suggest, may add substantially to the quality of interpersonal relationships and, thus, to the quality and academic effectiveness of middle school education as a whole. Since the teaching and learning experience in middle schools is interpersonal in its essence, these educators reason that student achievement, personal development, and group citizenship should all improve when pursued in a context of smallness that features long-term teacher-student relationships.

The sheer size that schools have become presents a problem in and of itself. Since consolidation began in the 1930s, the size of individual public schools has been increasing. In the years following World War II, however, school enrollments began to mushroom as the U. S. population experienced unprecedented growth. The major study of the status of middle level schools (McEwin, Dickinson, & Jenkins, 1996) charted their increasing size. When comparing 1968 data with 1986 data, the authors of the study noted little change in the percentage of middle schools enrolling 400 or fewer students, but in the five years between 1986 and 1993 there was a notable decrease in the percentage of such small schools. The percentage of middle schools with 401-800 students remained fairly constant from 1968 to 1993, but the percentage of middle schools with over 800 students increased rather dramatically from 16 percent to 30 percent during this period of 25 years (p. 16).

This trend toward much larger schools is of concern to most educators. Major efforts to create small schools were made in New York, Chicago, and Philadelphia as educators recognized that it was simply more difficult to create the kind of climate and learning environment that supports the academic and developmental goals of schools in large, impersonal institutions. Deborah Meier (1996), the creator of the innovative Central Park East Schools in New York City, in support of small schools has claimed

> Small schools come as close to being a panacea for America's educational ills as we're likely to get. Smallness is a prerequisite for the climate and culture that we need to develop the habits of the heart and mind essential to a democracy. Such a culture emerges from authentic relationships built on face-to-face conversations by people engaged in common work and common work standards. (p. 12)

The research supports such a position. The cumulative judgment of many studies is clear – smaller schools are more likely to be successful than larger ones. Although most of the research has been conducted at the elementary and high school levels, the strong consensus regarding the importance of smallness is applicable to the middle level. Student achievement, attendance, and participation in school activities, as well as parent involvement, are among the benefits that result from smallness. Studies also indicate the positive effects of small schools are greatest on minorities and students lower in socioeconomic status.

A new study reported in the *Atlanta Journal-Constitution* ("Study: Rich, Poor School Gap," 1999) supports this contention. The gap in academic achievement between rich and poor schools is far more pronounced, as much as 90 percent more, when schools are big than when they are small. Data compared scores on state tests with the poverty rate of 1,626 Georgia schools. The full study looked at the effects of school size, poverty, and achievement in Texas, Montana, and Ohio, as well as in Georgia. "The strongest point of the study is that the analysis was broad enough to show clearly that smaller schools are better for poorer kids than large schools," said Marty Strange, policy director of the Rural School and Community Trust, the Vermont-based organization that sponsored the research. While the study cannot say definitely why small is better for poor kids, Strange speculated that, "Poor kids don't have a way to get marginalized or pushed to the periphery in small schools" (p. G3).

The problems inherent in large schools have been exacerbated by social change. As schools have become more impersonal and anonymous because of their size, the gap between young adolescents and adults in their out-of-school time has been widening. Parents and other adults simply are spending less time in the company of youth. The anchors that family and neighborhood provided in earlier decades no longer exist. Young adolescents are now largely on their own in a world full of dangerous and readily available temptations. Probably no previous generation of adolescents has had so little guidance from adults or been more influenced by their peers. The public school, in order to fulfill its academic and broad educational responsibility, has begun to recognize this reality and respond by building into its regimen an atmosphere of caring that may begin with a breakfast program and an advisor-advisee program, and end with an after-school program. The metaphor "school as family" is apt and has become an acknowledged goal of many middle schools.

This book describes how to offer students the benefits of smallness within increasingly larger schools by ensuring long-term teacher-student relationships. Three major ways of achieving such relationships are discussed in some detail. A chapter presenting relevant research follows. The results of a national survey on long-term teacher-student relationships that includes the opinions of 105 educators, 586 parents, and 1,100 students from 33 schools comprise this study. Guidelines for practitioners interested in implementing long-term teacher-student relationships to make big schools seem small conclude this volume.

While still not common practice, it seems certain that increasing the time teachers and students spend together constitutes a bona fide trend. The simple logic of the concept, its compatibility with what is known about human growth and development, together with the increasing number of examples of successful implementation, bode well for this practice that seems so right for middle schools. And the frightening increase of school-based violence is causing educators and citizens generally to reassess the anonymity and alienation that too often characterize students' experiences in large middle and high schools. Smaller units that nurture long-term teacher-student relationships and counter feelings of anonymity or alienation may be a key factor in preventing school-related acts of violence. ∞

II
Long-Term Relationships and Middle School Students

The early adolescent years are widely recognized as a critical period in human development (Carnegie Council, 1989; George & Alexander, 1993; National Middle School Association, 1982, 1995). Middle school students experience profound mental, moral, social, sexual, emotional, and physical changes during the years from ten to fifteen. They also face the potential for substantial change in the quality and stability of their families, homes, peer groups, and economic status. In some ways, the lives of many young adolescents can be described as subject to constant change and continuing crisis, too often marked by shallowness and brevity in their relationships with others.

Organized and operated like smaller versions of high schools, traditional junior high schools and even many contemporary middle schools have added little to the quality or stability of students' relationships to teachers or peers. Students often are assigned to as many as eight different teachers and interact with hundreds of other students in a single day. Over a period of three or four years in a middle level school, some students may have classes with as many as 50 different teachers and be in short-term classes and other groups with hundreds, perhaps thousands, of different students. Combined with the pace of change in other areas of their personal and family lives, many middle school students' human relationships are like a high speed version of musical chairs punctuated by a "fruit basket turnover" each fall as new classes are formed.

Research in education and the social sciences demonstrates that young adolescents would benefit, in many ways, from greater stability in their relationships both with teachers and peers. Recent reform efforts, however, have focused largely on the "what" that is to be taught, and curricula are dutifully revised and prescribed in hopes of achieving the improved test scores that current calls for accountability demand. Overlooked is the "who" in the teaching-learning enterprise and how to enhance the influence of that "who." Although almost everyone knows instinctively that at the heart of successful teaching is a positive student-teacher relationship, educators often act as if they don't realize this and concern themselves almost exclusively with content, while all but ignoring the climate dictated by school size. Yet the hidden curriculum provides the context for the content curriculum and is a major determinant of its effectiveness.

The teacher ultimately is the most powerful influence in the classroom. To maximize the teacher's influence, it would seem that middle level schools ought to design programs that help to ensure a sense of smallness and increase opportunities for sets of teachers and students to be together longer. This is particularly relevant since middle level education has a special importance, one that is closely tied to the student-teacher relationship. During the middle school years young people make up their minds about the standards and values that will guide their behavior in adulthood. Teachers and parents are the most significant others in this critical period when attitudes and beliefs are formed. It is through people, what they do for them and with them, that youngsters learn who they are, what they can do, and what they should strive for. The middle level teacher is as much model as instructor, as much example as information source.

In a very real sense outstanding teachers achieve that distinction not so much because of the knowledge they possess or even the particular methods they employ, but because of who they are, their beliefs about themselves, teaching, and, of ultimate importance, their beliefs about students. In short-term fragmented relationships that influence is far less likely to be felt and certainly cannot be maximized.

The likelihood of teachers influencing students in ways that touch them and mold their behavior is far greater when they are working together over time rather than when their relationship is limited to formal instruction. Currently, it could be said, teachers are so busy teaching classes that they don't have time to direct the education of youth! The lessons that last, the ones that truly change behavior and become embedded in one's values and attitudes, are far more likely to result from the many little experiences and examples that arise out of living and working together than from any one class or series of formal lessons presented to a group. Significant learning that makes a difference in living is often the learning that is caught, not taught. Character, as the saying goes, resembles measles: it can only be caught by close contact with someone who has it. Today's students need time in the company of adults, larger amounts of time with fewer adults, working together in purposeful activities. Schools that provide small, closely-knit communities have, many believe, the best chance to prevent suicides and the kind of tragic violence witnessed in schools in recent years. Juvenile delinquents almost universally lack a bond with the school or with a teacher.

McLaughlin and Doda (1997), in a chapter aptly titled, "Teaching With Time on Your Side: Developing Long-Term Relationships in Schools," claimed: "Few would deny that time can offer amazing dividends in a teaching-learning context" (p. 57). And as you think about it, teaching in a very real sense is a matter of time – the time to answer a question, the time to listen, the time to offer support by one's presence, the time to remind and reinforce, the time to write a personalized note on a paper, the time to share in meaningful activities. Yes, teaching is really a matter of time, the time that it takes to influence youth both by instructing and modeling.

An interesting testament to the enduring importance of a meaningful teacher-student relationship was provided by Mark Springer (1994). Mark and his colleague, Ed Silcox, taught 40 seventh graders in a special program that was virtually an all-day, everyday integrated learning program built around the study of various aspects of life in the particular watershed where they were located. Mark provided this example (personal communication August 23, 1999):

> "Mr. Springer, would you be willing to write me a letter of recommendation for my college application?" On the surface, not an unusual request. Like countless other teachers throughout the country, I hear this request any number of times each fall as our high school seniors begin their quest for college admission. I always reply that I'd be glad to, and even though I know the answer, I ask, "Why me?" For unlike most teachers who are asked to write college admission letters, I don't teach high school students; I teach seventh graders. Invariably, the response comes, "Because you know me better than any of my high school teachers do."

Support for achieving long-term relationships

Support for the value of long-term relationships in school settings comes from many sources and scholars. For instance, what some scholars identify as social bonding theory (Hirschi, 1969) views student disengagement from school as a distinct danger to the natural developmental process young adolescents might follow. Students who do not form strong bonds in the school environment may end up dropping out of school or turning to some type of deviant behavior. Hirschi developed a theory of deviancy that connects delinquency to the weakening of a youth's bond to society. Young adolescents need to feel bonded to school, teachers, and peers. Recent school-based acts of violence only affirm this truism. Long-term relationships are one certain way to help students form and maintain the necessary links with society.

Hirschi (1969) also argued that persons without strong bonds were, not surprisingly, more likely to commit delinquent acts than those who were strongly bonded to traditional society. According to Hirschi, there are four elements that encourage a more positive social conformity: attachment, involvement, commitment, and belief. Attachment is defined as concern for the opinion of others; commitment is a rational decision to behave in acceptable ways related to gratification of immediate and long-term goals. Involvement is the expenditure of time and energy in institutionally encouraged behaviors, which precludes involvement in delinquent behaviors. Belief is a view that the principles encouraged by the institution are valid. Obviously, it is desirable for middle level schools to support the development of these elements of social bonding among the young adolescents whom they serve.

Social bonding theory leads directly to an educational variation, expressed in the theory of school membership (Wehlage, Rutter, Smith, Lesko, & Fernandez, 1989). Wehlage and associates described the theory of school membership this way:

> The theory hypothesizes school membership as the foundation upon which educational engagement is built. Interaction between these two concepts is indicated. Engagement and membership are shown as intermediate goals that schools must promote as a way of helping students arrive at the outcomes of achievement and personal and social development. (p. 279)

The theory of school membership states that successful students develop strong links to positive social groups within the school setting. School organization and management, unfortunately, can result in situations that impede the student's ability to socialize in ways that lead to positive school membership. In many middle level schools, students' social bonds are largely dismantled at the end of each school year, leaving each student challenged to form new social links with peers and teachers at the beginning of the next year.

Wehlage and associates (1989) argued that a lack of positive social bonding is an important factor involved in student choices related to success in school. For middle school students to be successful in school, and in later life, they need to be given the opportunity to develop strong and meaningful links with a positive,

11

durable, school-based social group. Students who experience positive long-term relationships are able to develop close peer groups, as well as connections to teachers, that last over several years. Long-term relationships of this sort provide students with the opportunity to develop satisfying interpersonal links, conditions that encourage the three goals of middle school education (George & Alexander, 1993): academic engagement, personal development, and group citizenship.

The theory of school membership states, further, that there are specific impediments to both academic engagement and group membership that can become the leverage points for practitioners who seek to improve student involvement. It is this notion of impediments that makes the theory helpful to practitioners, since, by identifying barriers to involvement, educators can focus on those conditions that block students' movement into membership and engagement (Wehlage et al., 1989, p. 279).

The practice of breaking up classes or teams each year and assigning students to different groups and new teachers is simply an impediment to membership. Often it takes a significant part of a school year for students to become comfortable within a group of students and teachers. As one teacher explained, "Just when students believe they are in a safe, supportive environment where they can take risks, the team is broken up and the process starts all over again the next year." Long-term relationships would permit students to remain in a familiar learning environment where impediments to membership are removed.

Works by Arhar (1992), Arhar & Kromrey (1993), and Kramer (1990) support middle school applications of the theory of school membership. Because of the failure of many families and communities to provide adequate opportunities for early adolescent social bonding and membership, the school becomes even more important as a locus for this developmental activity. And when these opportunities are not available at school, students may be at greater risk of dropping out and disengaging in other ways. Studies on why youth join gangs reveal that, for those youngsters, gangs are simply the best available means of having their developmental needs for identity, recognition, excitement, and security met – needs that a school can meet through long-term student-teacher relationships and collaboration.

Surely, then, when the school's organizational arrangements create a family atmosphere and enhance student-teacher relationships, the benefits for student engagement and involvement will be even greater. Single-year teaming can help students feel less alienated, but students have to start over each year and their potential sense of alienation is renewed on an annual basis. Young adolescents may be better served if they remain with the same group of teachers and students for two to three years or in other ways have continuing relationships with adults they know. Long-term relationships meet young adolescents' needs for attachment, involvement, continuity, and communality.

Positive long-term relationships help to create an affirming school environment, since, as Schmuck (1982) claims, the social-emotional tone of the school stems from the quality of the interpersonal relationships developed there. The social-emotional tone of a school affects whether or not students attend school, how effectively they will learn, and how they choose to behave while present. Teachers can establish in long-term relationships with students a positive social-emotional tone that lasts long enough to make a substantial difference in the quality of the school experience for everyone.

Often, middle school students feel lost in a large impersonal school so different from their elementary school, with alienation from school the result. Newmann (1981) stated that three human needs must be met to eliminate alienation: "the need for integration, or consistency and continuity in one's experience; the need for individuality; and the need for communality" (p. 549). Putting teams of students with "their" teachers is one way to help students develop a sense of belonging and feel the sense of community that Newmann describes (Arhar, 1992). Long-term teams, multiage grouping, and schools-within-a-school allow that sense of belonging and community to continue past one year, building a cumulative effect. Young adolescents quite typically feel a sense of alienation, but long-term relationships can counter that by helping students feel that they are an important part of an important group.

Newmann (1981) stated that teachers who define their role as more than classroom instructor and who spend a longer period with students are able to develop a closer, trusting relationship with students. Particularly as they enter a new and larger school, young adolescents need to know there is an adult who knows them well and in whom they can place their trust. This condition has been advocated across many years (Lounsbury & Vars, 1978; NMSA, 1995) and is typically made manifest in the form of a teacher advisory program. Such relationships allow students and teachers to form stronger, trusting bonds that exist apart from formal classroom instruction. Apparently middle schools generally have not suc-ceeded in establishing such relationships. Based on interviews and surveys of more than 4,200 parents and community members in nine states, researchers (Williamson & Johnston, 1999) identified anonymity as one of three major concerns. They concluded

> Middle schools were perceived by parents and other
> members of the community as impersonal and
> relatively anonymous places. Compared to most
> elementary schools, middle schools are substantially
> larger, and many buildings look and feel like large
> high schools. Parents perceived that even in the
> presence of teams and other organizational arrange-
> ments, their children were not known well by any
> single adult. (p. 10)

The more informal contacts of students and advisors over time, the greater the sense of communality and less the sense of alienation.

Long-term teacher-student relationships may have benefits directly related to academic outcomes, although debate continues about the effects of different versions of these arrangements on academic achievement (Veenman, 1995). Most reviews of previous research (McLaughlin, Irvin, & Doda, 1999) concluded that students in various grouping patterns leading to long-term relation-ships with teachers fared as well or better than students in standard age-grade classrooms, in terms of academic achievement on standardized tests. Affective outcomes, not surprisingly, are more favorably correlated to long-term teacher-student relationships (e.g., self-esteem, friendships). However, it should be noted, although not revealed in the paper and pencil test scores typically used to measure a school's success, these affective educational outcomes have more enduring importance in adult life. Research findings will be discussed more fully in Chapter IV.

Many of the most important goals of an education, it should be recognized, are difficult to achieve via a single course or within a single year. They require cumulative experiences and reflections over time. When together longer, teachers and students are able to focus on these longer-term academic goals and monitor progress over several years (George, 1987). It is particularly difficult to reach and teach within nine months those students who are, for whatever reasons, academically or attitudinally disadvantaged. Students need not begin every year with a new group of teachers unacquainted with their academic profiles, and time need not be devoted to a lengthy, time-consuming diagnosis of where the students are in the learning process. All too often, of course, time-pressed teachers may skip the entire process of diagnosis and simply begin the year wherever the scope and sequence chart suggests, regardless of student readiness. With long-term relationships persisting over the course of more than one academic year, the teacher and student may know more accurately where an entire team of students should begin its work at the start of the school year, in every facet of the curriculum.

If the students and teachers know they will be together the next year, it is less likely that the students will try, or be allowed, to slack off at the end of the year. Teachers can continue beyond their normal stopping point when spring fever usually takes over. In the same way, less time would be wasted at the beginning of each year. Time-on-task, which research proves is the most valuable commodity in producing academic achievement, is certain to benefit from teachers and students who view themselves as having a two- or three-year learning contract.

15

Information about students that teachers had internalized over the first year would be used in determining the educational needs of those students in subsequent years. Long-term relationships allow teachers to design curriculum that more accurately meet the individual needs of students they come to know so well. Students are more likely to see connections between subjects and topics over an extended period. In-depth, integrated curriculum experiences that go beyond merely correlating subjects are more easily developed in a team with long-term relationships. Teachers gain insights into many facets of their students' lives and are able to adapt both curriculum and instruction to reflect students' concerns and interests. This is in line with the curriculum integration movement slowly gaining favor. Beane (1997), a strong advocate of this major departure from traditional approaches, defines it in these terms:

> Curriculum integration is a curriculum design that is concerned with enhancing the possibilities for personal and social integration through the organization of curriculum around significant problems and issues, collaboratively identified by educators and young people, without regard for subject-area boundaries. (pp. x-xi)

While the potential gains to students in programs that provide long-term teacher-student relationships are more than sufficient to justify their creation, teachers gain, too. The significant benefits of such relationships to the teachers themselves should not be overlooked. When a teacher is responsible for directing a series of classes with 150 or more pupils in a day, that day can be hectic, stressful, and feel like a "rat race," as it is often characterized. The teacher's responsibility, in such situations, is primarily to instruct classes in the prescribed content – and when test scores reveal that students didn't master the content, frustration prevails. Teachers wonder if they are really making a difference. Their sense of efficacy and importance suffers. However, when teachers have more time with students, they not only know them better, they find greater satisfaction in their work. They have a sense that they are influencing individuals, meeting goals that

16

are of enduring importance. Multiage grouping, looping, and schools-within-a-school are organizational designs that support the commonly held belief that teachers who have more involvement with their students are more productive and more satisfied with their careers.

There are, then, a good many and quite varied reasons to implement organizational arrangements that create a sense of smallness and permit longer-term relationships between teachers and students, and among the students themselves. Academic engagement, positive personal development, and group citizenship may all develop more effectively in schools where students feel attached, involved, committed. When students and teachers invest in each other over a period of years, school membership leads to a more positive learning climate for all. Common sense and simple logic support long-term teacher-student relationships.

The research currently available on these organizational strategies and its correlation to educational outcomes is limited and even confusing, providing little guidance to practitioners. Much of the research is bogged down in the process of defining the variables clearly and describing research sites and situations with precision. While there is an urgent need for new qualitative and quantitative studies in this area, there is a strong professional consensus as to the validity of the concept of long-term teacher-student relationships. This consensus, backed up by increasing examples of successful practice, may be the best guidance available to practitioners – and professional consensus is a valuable and legitimate guide. ∞

III
Three Middle School Organizational Patterns

The vast majority of middle level schools are organized by grade level. Students, whether a part of a team or not, receive instruction from several teachers during the day and during the school year. The next year's schedule will likely put them under the guidance of a new set of teachers in different courses. This arrangement of organizing formal education in an age-segregated fashion is deeply embedded in American educational practice. Yet, upon honest analysis, it has to be recognized that apart from tradition and administrative convenience, there really is little to justify this or related practices. Although humans, as someone has noted, are not born in litters, we have somehow come to insist that they be educated in them.

Middle school educators have led the way in organizing interdisciplinary teams and have achieved considerable success in this deviation from traditional practice. Research has increasingly provided data that show the real and varied benefits of teaming (Flowers, Mertens, & Mulhall, 1999). However, these teams are usually organized by grade level, and students change teams each year; teaming, therefore, has not dramatically altered the overall institutional climate or the amount of time particular teachers and students spend together, although greatly increasing the possibilities of using that time more effectively.

There are three major organizational strategies now being used in middle level schools to achieve a sense of smallness within bigness and ensure long-term student-teacher relationships. No one of them is a new concept. In fact, two are connected to a much earlier era in our history, and the third was a widely touted innovation in the late 1950s and 1960s.

The first strategy is multiage grouping, a practice that places students from two or more grades together in the same classroom. This practice, reminiscent of the one-room school, has been freshened up and presented as a new idea. It has been viewed with considerable skepticism, however, in spite of the research support the practice has garnered (Lloyd, 1999). The age-grade organizational pattern has been universally practiced for so long it has been institutionalized, so the notion of organizing a multigrade classroom is viewed as a radical idea. However, on examination it becomes apparent that with rare exception, every middle level classroom is, in fact, multiage.

A check of two randomly selected middle school homerooms in a central Georgia school, for instance, revealed that as of August 1, 1999, in a typical seventh grade homeroom of 27 pupils there was an 11 year-old, a 14 year-old, three 13 year-olds, and twenty-two 12 year-olds. In an eighth grade homeroom of 26 pupils, there were three 14 year-old students and two 12 year-olds along with the majority of 13 year-olds. The assumption that students at a particular grade level are about the same chronological age is false. (If the variance of a class on measures of achievement were charted, an even far greater range of differences would be apparent.) The multiage classroom at the middle level, it appears, is already standard practice. And, of course, multiage grouping is regularly practiced in band, chorus, and athletic activities without any reservations.

The second strategy, also reminiscent of the one-room school, is the student-teacher progression plan, now most commonly called looping. It involves keeping a team of middle level teachers with the same group of students for more than one year, thus ensuring a sense of family. Looping has been frequently employed at the elementary level, but is now gaining a strong following at the middle level, where it can counter the effects of schools that have become too large.

The third strategy, a somewhat less intensive alternative, is the schools-within-a-school organization that divides a too-large school into smaller schools or houses where students spend their entire middle school experience in the same area of the building under the direction of the same faculty. Students, however, are likely to be taught by different teams from one year to the next but would be acquainted with the individual school's faculty and feel connected to a relatively small student body and its faculty.

Most Americans are familiar with the old saying that "necessity is the mother of invention." Middle school educators are inventive by nature and likely to respond to current educational necessities by creating new and more effective methods for making big schools feel small. Here, we document and describe three such educational strategies already in place.

1. MULTIAGE GROUPING

Multiage grouping in middle schools is an organizational strategy in which students of different ages, ability levels, and interests are intentionally placed together on the same team. Typically, each multiage team represents the school in microcosm. In a multiage-grouped middle school with grades six, seven, and eight, for example, each team may have one-third of its students from each of the three grades. In such a case, at the end of each year one-third of the students (eighth graders) leave for high school to be replaced in the fall with a one-third contingent of sixth graders. Another distinguishing feature of multiage grouping is the fact that students from different grade levels remain not only in the same house or on the same team, but that they frequently are grouped within their classes without regard to grade level. Students remain with the team of students and teachers for three years, beginning and ending their middle school careers on the same team. This arrangement tends to make the overall size of the total school a non-factor.

Over 25 years ago Lincoln Middle School, in Gainesville, Florida, provided an excellent example of multiage grouping

(George, 1987). When it opened in the early 1970s, under the pioneering leadership of principal John Spindler, each of the six interdisciplinary teams at Lincoln contained five teachers and approximately 150 students, 50 each from the sixth, seventh, and eighth grades. Each teacher had primary responsibility for one subject and taught students on the same team from three grade levels. The teachers and students remained together for three years; each year the eighth graders were replaced by a new group of sixth graders. Each heterogeneous team reflected the composition of the total school population; each team was a Lincoln in microcosm.

The operation of this arrangement at this innovative school was fairly straightforward. In mathematics, reading, and language arts, students were diagnosed, placed, and taught via a form of cross-grade ability grouping for the three years they were on the team. In heterogeneously grouped social studies and science classes, a three-year cycle insured that every student received all three years of the curriculum in each subject by the time he/she departed for the high school. At the same time, the cross-grade ability grouping worked so that teachers were confronted with a reasonable range of achievement levels in each of their classes. In fact, this appears to be one version of the few grouping processes which generally defy the negative outcomes to which most variations of tracking are prone (Slavin, 1989).

Multiage grouping, as employed in the example above, reduced the number of students a teacher had to get to know, and vice versa. At the same time, it extended each of these interpersonal relationships to a length that was triple those achieved in conventional arrangements. A teacher in a middle school with traditional grade level grouping would teach approximately 450 different students over three years; conversely, a teacher on a multiage four-teacher team might have approximately 250 students over three years. With a major reduction in the number of students a teacher has to get to know and greatly increased time with those students, teachers would be able to develop close relationships with students and better get to know students' individual needs. The same benefits, of course, also accrue to students and parents. Today, educators might imagine what the addition of a large block schedule might have contributed to the intensity of the teacher-student relationship.

In a study of Lincoln Middle School, George (1987) noted a number of barriers to the realization of appropriate school goals were eliminated by the multiage grouping process. Teams avoided those common problems associated with similar tracking and ability grouping systems employed elsewhere. Discipline inside and outside the classroom became much less of a problem when teachers and students maintained their relationships for three years. Beginnings and endings of the year, in particular, were much smoother. Parent relationships and the conferences that developed out of them were much more positive and productive. Interethnic relationships improved measurably. Teachers, students, parents, and administrators discovered that several dozen school processes were very efficient and effective when the "promise of permanence" was introduced into the structure of interpersonal relationships in the school.

Some curriculum adaptations are necessary for multiage grouping to function smoothly, but it does not require that each teacher teach three different grade level lessons in each class each day. Teachers recoil, rightly, at the thought of being responsible for teaching world history, American history, and geography in the same class to three different groups. This is not what happened at Lincoln.

The basic academic program at Lincoln was modified in two ways. Mathematics, language arts, and reading were frequently arranged in cross-grade ability groups, so that students worked on specific objectives or tasks appropriate for them. Students moved from objective to objective or from skill to skill, and were grouped and regrouped over a period of three years as they demonstrated mastery or completed a particular set of activities. So, students could have joined a team in sixth grade, or at any other point, and moved along steadily from one year to the next. Students were diagnosed, placed, taught, assessed, and regrouped in a continuing cycle.

In social studies and science, the curriculum was arranged on a three-year cycle. Based on the credible assumption that there was very little inherent sequence in learning either of these two subject areas, entire teams of students studied a particular aspect of the curriculum during the same year, regardless of the age or grade of the students. In social studies, students on two teams might have, for example, studied American history during year A, world history during year B, and geography during the year C of the cycle. Two other teams would study world history during year A, and the final two teams would study geography during year A. In science, the rotation of the cycle would be similar.

It is important to note that, for new students, placement on a multiage team at Lincoln usually involved very little difficulty. Since everything major in the curriculum was always being taught on some team in the school, students were placed on the team that most nearly matched the program they had been following in their previous school. This situation also prevented excessive strain on library and other resources for any particular subject.

Mebane Middle School, in Alachua, Florida, may have been, at one point, the most flexibly grouped middle school in America. In operation since 1970, during most of the decade from 1975 to 1985, Mebane had approximately 460 students in grades five through eight. The school had three multiage-grouped teams, each containing approximately 40 students from every grade level, five through eight. Students remained on the team, then, for four years.

At Mebane, the student population on each team changed by one quarter each year. The eighth graders moved on to the high school, and fifth graders moved in from the elementary school. The team or "learning community," as the faculty called it, remained about 75 percent whole each year. Within each team at Mebane, special grouping for instruction further accommodated the characteristics of the students on the team.

In reading and mathematics, students on the teams at Mebane were divided by ability into two large groups. One group was composed of middle to high ability students, the second contained middle to low ability students. Half of the students studied the basic skills in the morning, half in the afternoon. Since the grouping disregarded grade levels, it was common for students from at least three grade levels to be together in class. Such a program permitted regrouping for mathematics in much the same way that grouping was done for reading.

In science and social studies, and in physical education and pre-vocational classes, students were grouped without rigid ability or achievement level criteria but with an attempt to reduce the instructional range. Within each team, students were grouped as follows: fifth and sixth graders together, sixth and seventh, seventh and eighth graders, and occasionally at least three grade levels were in class together if student characteristics or needs suggested it. Curriculum units were repeated every other year, avoiding duplication for students.

Perhaps the best-known and most progressive multiage team is the Alpha Team of the Shelburne Community School in Shelburne, Vermont. In operation since 1972, Alpha began as an alternative for the more traditional interdisciplinary team in that school. What has really set it apart, however, is not just its multiage composition but its fully integrated curriculum and student-directed practices, with objectives that go well beyond the usual coverage of content. There is no set scope or sequence of subjects to be covered in a cycle, as in the case of Lincoln. The curriculum is created by the students and teachers working in collaboration.

Sixth, seventh, and eighth graders assigned to Alpha Team work under the direction of three highly competent teachers. Carol Smith (1999), who has been on that team for 24 years, believes the multiage approach is especially valuable because it provides "continuity of program, practice, and expectations, growth over time, shared history, and strong relationships with students and families." To her, the artificial, single year divisions imposed in schools have little to do with learning and certainly nothing to do with children and their growth.

Alpha Team strives to be a true community of learners, a variety of ages working together, learning with and from each other just as "real-life" communities do. Students on the Alpha Team are organized into three multiage prime groups. Each group is guided by one Alpha teacher who monitors and supports individual progress throughout the year. This yearlong prime group organization provides a consistent framework for developing strong student-teacher relationships and fostering close family connections. Goal setting and assessment are part of each week. Students work with a goals partner and their prime teacher to set appropriate goals (many based on a current theme or project) and then assess those goals at the end of the week. Weekly goals provide the road map for how students plan their time both in school and at home. A daily morning meeting outlines the master schedule of group activities, and then students designate time for individual work on their schedules. Students move purposefully from one activity to another, each according to his/her own plan. Students take on as much responsibility for their own planning and scheduling as they are ready to assume. It is only over time and with practice that goal setting and scheduling become an automatic part of managing time.

Carol Smith (personal communication, June 9, 1999) describes effectively the way the three-year span of time provides for student growth and participation in the following paragraphs:

> Students of various ages have the opportunity to try on a variety of roles as they become ready to do so. Older students help younger students, and quite often, younger students emerge as leaders as well.
>
> Our team is family-like, with oldest, youngest, and middle children all at the same time. For each child there is the chance to take on each of those roles and move out of his/her family designation. We believe this gives students a wider perspective of themselves and others, offering students greater chances to succeed in a wider variety of ways.
>
> Being the "youngest child" gives students permission to ask a lot of questions, rely on others, watch how others do things, try new things, make mistakes in a safe environment, and know there is

time to try again. This first year is truly a time to learn.

The "middle child" has the rare gift of time to practice. He/she knows the systems and procedures of the team, has watched how it is done, and now can practice all the things introduced the year before. Being successful at some of the things that gave difficulty the year before is exhilarating and self-affirming. Students get to use their understanding of the team to help the new students, while holding their *safe* "in the middle" place. Leadership opportunities present themselves when students are ready and pave the way for the following last year.

As the "oldest," in their eighth grade year, students have now risen to the top of the three-year cycle and are the leaders they have learned to be. This year offers many opportunities to work in partnership with the teachers, be role models for others, and pass on the legacy that is Alpha to the others. Students in the eighth grade have become the "oldest" in a very real and natural way – learning, practicing, modeling, and teaching as they have grown into the role of "oldest."

The team cultivates a family environment through a number of team traditions. For example, eighth graders and teachers spend a day together before school starts. This "eighth graders only" retreat gives them a chance to reconnect and explore their roles as student leaders and teachers as well as reminisce about their journey together. They also plan sixth grade orientation activities. Another tradition occurs at the end of the year when eighth graders tell the Alpha "story" to the seventh graders and pass the role of "oldest" on to the next group. Students have come to realize what it means to be an Alpha student and want to share their personal and collective understandings of the teams in some symbolic way and pass them on.

In support of the concept of Alpha Team as a true learning community, students are expected to participate in decisions made about what and how they learn. The team, in concert, literally creates its own curriculum. Themes are drawn from student questions and concerns, and knowledge and skills from the disciplines are repositioned into the context of these themes. Through all aspects of the program, students work to develop and understand their personal learning styles, reflect and report in formal ways on what they have learned, and consciously plan their next steps. The team believes in empowering students to take the initiative, think for themselves, and assume responsibility for their own learning. Learning to make decisions and accept the consequences are integral parts of the Alpha experience. Democracy demands active and informed participation. "The way to teach democracy is to practice it," Smith states simply. "Twice a year students conduct their own parent conferences, sharing their portfolios and setting goals. Daily morning meetings are supplemented by a weekly Class Meeting, a forum organized and run by students."

The varied and extensive roles of an Alpha teacher have been described by Smith (1999) in these terms: "guide, coach, role model, leader, colleague, partner, learner, evaluator, manager, counselor, instructor, friend, disciplinarian, mentor, observer, organizer, peacemaker, tutor, surrogate parent, historian, advocate, educator, worker, visionary – often all in the same day" (p. 2).

Reflecting on her years as the lead teacher of the Alpha Team, Carol Smith (personal communication, June 9, 1999) penned these comments that make evident the value to both students and faculty of having a small unit with long-term student-teacher relationships:

> For me, the relationship I build with students and families is the icing on the cake of teaching on this three-year multiage team. I have been given the luxury of time with these kids and with families to let learning happen in a more natural way. These students have had time and opportunity to learn about themselves, to celebrate their successes, and to

understand their challenges. They know themselves well. The three years on the Alpha Team has been an instrumental part of their journey and they are ready to move on. I am confident that they will succeed. They are strong and powerful young people ready and able to take on the challenges of high school. What a gift it is to have these three years with them.

Eggers Middle School, in Hammond, Indiana, has used multiage grouping for a long time, although not in as progressive a manner as Alpha. Having been organized into interdisciplinary teams since 1976, the Eggers staff moved to multiage grouping "to assist in more effectively addressing the sociological, developmental, and academic needs of the early adolescent." Students are assigned to one of three heterogeneous "Learning Communities" for the length of the educational program through grades six through eight. Each Learning Community is identified by a color. Each has approximately 250 students and 10 teachers in these areas: language arts, reading, foreign language, math, science, social studies, and special education. Teams (Learning Communities) have block schedules that permit 90 minutes of daily planning, conferencing, and meetings. Much of this time is devoted to what the Eggers staff calls "community coordination." Since each Learning Community at Eggers has the same students for three years, teachers tend to engage in considerably more "pupil personnel services" during their "community coordination" time.

Two exemplary Midwestern middle schools have used multiage grouping in large schools where only two grades are present (George & Alexander, 1993). At Trotwood-Madison Junior High School in Trotwood, Ohio, 850 students have been divided into four teams each containing an equal number of seventh and eighth grades. Each team has five teachers and an aide. At Brentwood Middle School in Greeley, Colorado, the school has been divided into six teams of between 100 and 140 sixth- and seventh-grade students, with three to four teachers on each team. At Brentwood, the instructional groupings in the subject areas were based on diagnosed instructional need without regard to student age or ability. Thus, the sixth and seventh graders are mixed in all classes.

Another remarkably different version of multiage grouping exists at Brown Barge Middle School in Pensacola, Florida. At Brown Barge, teachers and students are organized into what educators there call "streams," teams of teachers and approximately 150 sixth, seventh, and eighth graders – all of whom have chosen to study a particular theme for a period of 12 weeks. Students and teachers are grouped without regard to grade level, in response to their desire to study one of four themes (e.g., arts motifs) that are being offered during that trimester. Stream topics change each trimester, so groups of teachers and students are reorganized three times each year. Over the period of three years that students spend at Brown Barge, however, particular teachers and students will likely study together again and again.

As the practice of multiage grouping spreads, a number of educators have found that offering this form of grouping in addition to continued use of some chronological age grouping, in the same school setting, makes an effective transitional strategy. Choices may then be offered to parents, students, and teachers as to which style of grouping they prefer. Under such circumstances all groups feel considered and well served, and a seemingly controversial grouping strategy is implemented with little or no turmoil.

Several varieties and styles of such combinations are in operation around the country. At Louisville Middle School in Louisville, Colorado, fifth and sixth graders were combined for instruction in mathematics, language arts, reading and exploratory options, but were taught by grade levels in science and physical education. Seventh and eighth graders work together only in elective areas, except during the extensive activity period when students from grades five through eight are grouped together. This method of interweaving multiage grouping and chronological age grouping is likely to receive support from everyone concerned.

At Nipher Middle School in Kirkwood, Missouri, parents and students are offered some choices in a school containing grades six through eight. A self-contained sixth-grade option is available, as well as two- and four-teacher teams; eighth graders all work in interdisciplinary teams. In between, there is an option of a two-year sixth- to seventh-grade multiage-grouped situation. Materials distributed to parents by the principal explain that the sixth- to seventh-grade team follows a two-year curriculum that incorporates materials from both years. Students would be expected to be on the team for two years.

At Noe Middle School in Louisville, Kentucky, multiage grouping was introduced to the school gradually, one team at a time. Everyone involved, and particularly teachers, had a chance to become familiar with the concept of having sixth, seventh and eighth graders on the same team. Initially, the students in the school were grouped according to age and grade level. Then a team of volunteer teachers and a selected group of students became a multiage-grouped unit. After a year's successful operation, a second team switched to the multiage format, and the next year a third team changed over. By the 1979-80 year, there were three multiage and three graded teams at Noe. Eventually, all teams were multiaged. Regrettably, over a period of years, changes transpired that, by 1992, resulted in multiage grouping operating in only one team.

In 1993, the leadership team of Crabapple Middle School in Fulton County, Georgia, launched an investigation of alternative models. Concerned that the school had settled into a routine, even regressed somewhat, the team sought a project that would energize the school and improve student learning. After reading, discussing, and visiting other schools, the multiage grouping concept emerged as the one with the greatest promise. Two multiage teams were launched that fall with assistance from an ESEA Title III Grant. Heterogeneous teams of sixth, seventh, and eighth graders were selected with both gifted and special education students included. The teachers, students, and parents all made a three-year commitment to the program. The many benefits attributed to such programs cited earlier proved to be present in the case of Crabapple.

Linda Hopping (1999), the recently retired principal of Crabapple, enthusiastic about the experience, claimed

> The implementation and subsequent success of the
> multiage program was the highlight of my career as a
> middle school administrator. It embodied the very
> best of the middle school: a child-centered approach
> to educating the preadolescent; challenging curricu-
> lum with enrichment opportunities far beyond those
> available in the regular classroom; hands-on inte-
> grated learning; individualized instruction at all
> levels; an emphasis on the development of critical
> thinking skills; cooperative group work; natural
> advisory programs; a feeling of "family" or commu-
> nity; conflict resolution and character education;
> opportunities for success for each child regardless
> of ability; and student and teacher empowerment.
> (p. 4)

Parents were actively involved in the Crabapple multiage
teams through Family Councils where parents met with teachers to
help plan and facilitate instruction. Adversarial positions were rare,
and the mutual cooperation between school and home provided
students with a secure and consistent support system. The inclusion
of several components of Project Adventure proved to be major
determinants of the program's success.

A three-year rotational cycle similar to that at Lincoln was
employed in social studies and language arts with students from the
three grade levels grouped together. In mathematics and science,
however, groups were established primarily by skill level. Teachers,
students, and parents all found this curriculum arrangement to be
very satisfactory.

The long-term relationships made it possible to meet many
individual needs that would not likely be served in a traditional
one-year setting. For example, a boy who experienced difficulty in
math was being tutored by another boy on the team. By Christmas,
real progress was apparent. At winter break the mother of the boy
who was doing the tutoring and who knew nothing of her son's
mentoring questioned him when she read a card with this message:
"Thank you for caring. I never could have made it without you."

Not the typical message between two young adolescent boys, but it was typical of the level of caring and support among students on the team. Another boy visited the high school where he understood a great many ninth graders were having difficulty making the transition into the high school. Following that visit, he and several of his classmates developed a program called "Bridges," which addressed transition issues and soon became a model for the entire district.

Another student, a girl who was classified as learning disabled always felt she was "different." She hated to go out for fire drills with her special education class where others would see her. When placed on the multiage team she received her individualized program within the team. The day of the first fire drill she ran home and told her mother, "We had a fire drill today and it was okay because I am not different anymore."

The multiage teams at Crabapple Middle School offered a much richer, broader experience wherein in-depth exploration and active learning were ongoing. At the same time discipline problems all but disappeared, attendance improved, skills were mastered as they were used in functional ways, creativity surfaced, and varied instructional strategies were used. The ultimate success of the program, as is usually the case in any reform effort, was closely related to the teachers and their willingness to go beyond normal expectations. But, Linda Hopping (1999) notes, for those willing, it is the most rewarding experience of their educational careers.

An interesting development occurred in Cobb County, Georgia, in 1998 ("Makeshift Cobb School," 1999), where serious overcrowding forced officials to place in one building ninth graders from a high school and eighth graders from two middle schools. Parents weren't happy; neither were students. But when the first year of this emergency arrangement ended, school officials were stunned. The failure rate for ninth graders was among the lowest in the county and far lower than expected. Students spoke of getting to know one another and bonding. Eighth graders were not negatively influenced by ninth graders, and ninth graders enjoyed and seemed to profit from the presence of eighth graders.

Multiage advisory programs

A variation of the multiage classroom group is the multiage advisory group. Based on the same principles and purporting to have essentially the same benefits, multiage advisory groups, while still scarce, have been in practice in a number of schools for many years. An advisory group would be composed of five or six sixth graders, and a like number of seventh and eighth graders. The advisor remains with the group so that any one student has a three-year relationship with that adult advocate. When the eighth graders graduate, they are replaced by sixth graders. The entering sixth graders are able to benefit from having the guidance of seventh and eighth graders in a setting that avoids much of the taunting associated with being "freshmen."

The Wantagh Middle School in Wantagh, New York, has operated a very successful multiage advisory program for a number of years. Dr. Jeannette Stern (personal communication, December 12, 1999), cochair of the Advisory Council that developed and oversees the program, characterizes it as "a home away from home." The program seeks to achieve the same goals as most advisory programs, and it rests on the same philosophical basis. The particular advantages of the multiage advisory are well stated in a school brochure.

Why Multigrade Advisory?

Having a multigrade organization to advisory fills a number of additional needs in the building. The integration of new students into the building is accomplished more quickly and more efficiently as everyone plays a part, including the other students in advisory. In the spring, letters are sent from members of the existing sixth grade advisees to the incoming advisees welcoming them to the building and their advisory. Each student in advisory that first week takes a personal interest in ensuring that the new students feel at home.

Reduction/elimination of intergrade conflicts is another advantage of the multigrade advisory program. Students are immediately part of a multiage "family" type atmosphere, the sixth versus seventh versus eighth grade mischief prevalent in other schools disappears and an older brother- and sister-type atmosphere appears. Younger students have no second thoughts about asking for directions, help with a difficult locker, or homework questions. Older students offer "scholarly" tips and test others in material they have already mastered. At times, the younger students with skills in specific areas come to the aid of the older students as well.

Teachers have an increased awareness of the developmental needs of all middle level youngsters. They see the need for differentiating teaching techniques, have a firsthand knowledge of vertical and horizontal articulation of subject and program, and regardless of their individual role in the building, have the opportunity to develop a three-year relationship with their "own" students.

Teachers provide support for each other through Advisory Support Groups. These function as advisory for advisors, providing the opportunity for sharing of "what works" strategies, evaluating informally the progress of the program, and suggesting new activities.

The Wantagh advisory program also follows a particularly interesting practice. On normal days a ten-minute advisory period opens the school's schedule supplemented by an extended advisory period every other Friday. On the very first day of school in the fall, however, the advisory period lasts a full hour. Here the seventh and eighth graders welcome the new sixth graders. After getting acquainted they help them work locker combinations, understand the computerized schedule, locate various classrooms, restrooms, and other school-wide facilities. The sixth graders leave school at the end of that first day with a few friends in all three grades. The previous spring, individual sixth graders write to a fifth grader who will join the advisory group. Often an exchange of letters or phone calls between the two follow, and sometimes they arrange to meet.

Dr. Stern reports that the multigrade format has brought the entire building together and formed a cohesive student body. Teachers and parents enjoy and approve of the multi-year commitment and continuity. As a result of the Wantagh's experience, many flourishing spin-off programs have been set up in Long Island. In Talent Middle School in Talent, Oregon, the practice of multiage advisory groups has been in operation for many years. Advisors there also serve as facilitators for the school-wide, semi-annual, student-led parent conferences.

Schools not able or ready to institute multiage teams for academic instruction may want to consider establishing their advisory program on the multiage basis. The logic is obvious.

2. LOOPING

The practice of keeping a teacher and a class together for two or three years has come to be known as looping. Like multiage grouping it is a throwback to the one-room school where, of necessity, a student might spend an entire elementary career under the direction of one teacher. Sometimes called teacher rotation, teacher cycling, or student-teacher progression, it has been practiced at the elementary level for many decades. Grant, Richardson, and Forsten (2000) note that

> A 1913 memo from the U.S. Department of the Interior (back in the days when there was no federal agency responsible for public education) touted looping as one of the most important issues facing urban schools: "Shall teachers in graded schools be advanced from grade to grade with their pupils through a series of two, three, four, or more years so that they may come to know the children they teach and be able to build the work of the latter

years on that of the earlier years, or shall teachers be required to remain year after year in the same grade while the children, promoted from grade to grade, are taught by a different teacher every year? This I believe to be one of the most important questions of city school administration." (p. 2)

Two years later the Bureau of Education in the Department of the Interior (1916) issued Bulletin 1915, No. 42, *Advancement of the Teacher with the Class*. Written by a high school English teacher, this 81-page publication reported on a survey of 813 superintendents regarding this topic. The report noted that "an unfortunate application of the doctrine of efficiency has led to the mechanical, unprogressive assignment of teachers. The result is that a teacher, once assigned to a grade...remains commonly fixed in that grade, on the grounds that she knows the work better than any other work, and can therefore do it better" (p. 7).

The report presented from a theoretical standpoint the case for having teachers advance to another grade with students and made these rather intriguing claims:

On general grounds, in accordance with the principles of pedagogy and psychology, the argument is strong for the advancement of the teacher with her pupils for a considerable period of time. The personality of the teacher is the vitalizing force in education, and it is productive in individuals (a) according to native endowment, (b) according to personal training and attainment in knowledge, sympathy, and skill. When a wholesome, productive personality has once begun to stimulate into new life and power the growing, conscious being of the child, its activity should be continued so long as it shows a normal quickening influence. This is essential for conscious mental unity in the child, and for normal, uniform development. Mental motherhood is as much a fact as physical motherhood, as every teacher knows, and should be needlessly disturbed as little in the one case as in the other, at least until under the stimulating influence, the inchoate personality of the child begins to unfold its independent powers. When this mental motherhood, with its resulting intimate acquaintance, is once productively established, it should not only occasion a saving of time, but many other advantages should result, to the city, State, and Nation through the teacher's more vital contact with the child and his home, and her consequent greater ability to help him adjust himself to life. It should follow, also, that inopportune change of personal influence, particularly in the earlier stages of self-realization, would lead to faults and distortions, mental, moral and spiritual. (pp. 8-9)

The report presented detailed responses of superintendents and teachers on the merits of the plan. Reports from foreign schools also led to the still true judgment that "the advancement plan has been more extensively applied in foreign countries than in the United States" (p. 56). The overall conclusion of the survey was that administrators and teachers generally supported the theory but raised a variety of objections that kept implementation at a low level.

Despite this advocacy from the Bureau of Education, the concept of advancing pupils with their teacher remained rather dormant for over half a century. In the late 1980s, this practice gained relatively widespread attention at the elementary level and even some implementation at the middle level. The benefits that arise from long-term relationships are manifold and quite obvious. Jim Grant (1998), a strong advocate of both looping and multiage grouping, has claimed that there are 17 specific benefits to looping and that "it is the best element of the one-room schoolhouse that valued teachers and students having a long-term relationship." When a team continues with a group of students in a single grade for another year, it has been said they receive "the gift of time" and benefit from an extra month of instruction – that first month in the second year that is usually taken up with getting acquainted with a new group of students, diagnosing their achievement status, and working out procedures. Some even claim there is a second extra month, the last month of the first year when students remain accountable to the team they know they will have in the fall rather than slacking off. However, looping, like teaming, only provides opportunities for teachers to improve education; the structure itself does not automatically yield benefits, although it sets the stage for change.

Given the positive experiences wherever it has been practiced, it is somewhat surprising that looping has not yet become a more common organizational arrangement. Almost any teacher can quickly enumerate the possible benefits of having this kind of long-term relationship. With few disadvantages to offset the many common-sense advantages, one might conclude that the biggest barrier may be just the deeply embedded and institutionalized practice of single grade, single year grouping wherein a teacher is viewed as a fifth grade teacher or a sixth grade teacher or, even more narrowly circumscribed as a seventh grade math teacher or an eighth grade language arts teacher. As Grant and colleagues (2000) point out

> The notion of finding a new dentist or physician each year for every child seems absurd. We want children to know their doctors and to feel comfortable with them. It is important for physicians to know their patients as they grow and develop. Yet for many of these same children, their schools assign them to a new teacher and require they learn a new set of classroom routines and adult expectations every year. (pp. 3-4)

At Lincoln Middle School, in Gainesville, Florida, after a decade of successful multiage grouping described earlier in this chapter, the district school board (for reasons having little to do with middle school) developed a ruling which made it impossible for the staff to continue the practice. The reaction of the faculty and administrators, who had come to realize the tremendous power of the long-term team process that they were about to lose, was to search for another version which the school board would permit. Student-Teacher-Progression, as they labeled it, resulted (George, 1987).

The faculty and staff of Lincoln, after considerable discussion, arrived at a consensus that brought them to reorganize their interdisciplinary teams so that three-year teams of a different sort emerged. For the next half dozen years or more, the teams were organized by grade level: two teams at each grade level, six through eight. Teams of teachers who began a year with sixth grade students stayed with that group of students for three years, through the end of the eighth grade, at which time they would rotate back to pick up a new cohort of sixth graders. This looping process, while less popular with the staff at Lincoln than multiage grouping, delivered many of the same benefits of multiage grouping. In the fall of 1991, one teacher from Lincoln recalled her last year there as "the pinnacle of my teaching career" because it coincided with the last year of the three-year cycle with the same students (George, 1987).

Sue Kowalski (personal communication, January 4, 2000), a teacher at the Frazier School in Syracuse, New York, was part of a three-person team that has practiced looping for four years. The following reflections of her experience on looping incorporate many of the generally recognized advantages of this practice.

> We keep, by design, our students for 7th and 8th grade. For reasons that I have finally figured out aren't just coincidental, the second year we are together is much closer to "poetry in motion" than the first year. Initially, I dreaded the thought of having to teach an entirely new curriculum, deal with the same kids for another year, and truly believed I was being deprived of the opportunity of that annual September fresh start.

> How incredibly naive I was! One day into our second year of the "loop," I knew this was a beautiful thing. Traditional beginning-of-the-year talks about expectations and guidelines were now just reminders rather than setting forth a new set of rules. An atmosphere of trust was there, and though I can't guarantee every student felt 100% secure, my hunch was most everyone had let his guard down. Students had not only matured chronologically, but

a true team had been formed. When I finally felt like things were coming together in May of 7th grade, I knew I had a whole year ahead of me to take it to the next level. We could actually see the results of our hard work, not just wonder what had "taken."

As a teacher I love it. I don't see it as teaching two separate curriculums, but rather making logical connections from where we left off. I don't see it as more work, but rather a two-year program where I am not forced to do the same thing every year. I am able to make connections with students that help me understand them as a person, not just as a student. I know so much about some students that we can have conversations based on trust and not just on topics that happened to surface in our short time together in class. We know parents better and have a better understanding of our wide array of families; we learn what works and what doesn't; we know who can come to school and who can't. We build family relationships as well.

One of Kowalski's students, Ashley, expressed in these sentences what was a fairly typical student reaction to looping.

I like looping. I think it is a good idea that you stay with your teacher for two years because you grow and become closer with friends and teachers and that's important because if you have a problem then you won't feel that shy to talk to a teacher about it because you've known them. You get to know people better and become friends with people who you thought you didn't like because you really didn't know them.

At Mandarin Middle School, in Duval County, Florida, 2,400 students were organized into three houses of 800 students; each house contained five or six interdisciplinary teams of approximately 150 students and four teachers in each. At Mandarin, teachers and parents have a choice about whether to belong to a regular team, with a new set of teachers and students each year, or to what school leaders call a "progression" team. On progression teams, teachers and students remained together for three years, throughout the students' tenure at Mandarin. Teams formed with new students in the sixth grade and continued with them until the students left for high school.

A number of other middle schools have implemented aspects of the student teacher progression or looping model: Pittsford Middle School in Pittsford, New York; Campbell Drive Middle School in Homestead, Florida; Westview Middle School in Longmont, Colorado; and Skowhegan Middle School in Skowhegan, Maine, are four dramatically different locations, with very different student demographics, where educators decided that a version of looping works for them and their students.

At Skowhegan Middle, containing only grades seven and eight, there were five teams of teachers and students; each team stayed together for the two years the students were in the school. Each team was heterogeneously grouped, and all special education and gifted students were completely mainstreamed on these teams. In an evaluation of the two-year relationship, the following conclusions were reported (Lynch, 1990):

- Ninety-two percent of the staff agreed or strongly agreed that this approach results in our students receiving a better education.

- Ninety-six percent of the staff agreed or strongly agreed that this approach resulted in the team's having a better understanding of the individual student.

- Ninety-six percent of the staff agreed or strongly agreed that this approach resulted in better parent communication and cooperation.

- Ninety-one percent of the staff agreed or strongly agreed that these organizational changes have made our students more enthusiastic about learning.

Westview Middle School may have been the first school to implement looping in a brand new building and program, doing so during the 1991-92 school year. Bob Moderhak, then principal of Westview, cites David and Roger Johnson (1989) for support for this way of providing long-term relationships:

> School has to be more than a series of "shipboard romances" that last for only a semester or year. In this and a number of other ways schools act as if relationships are unimportant. Each semester or year, students get a new set of classmates and a new teacher. The assumption seems to be that classmates and teachers are replaceable parts and any classmate or any teacher will do. The result is that students have a temporary one-semester or one-year relationship with classmates and the teacher.
>
> Relationships do matter. Caring and committed relationships are a major key to school effectiveness, especially for at-risk students who often are alienated from their families and society....Classrooms and schools need to be caring communities in which students care about each other and are committed to each other's well being....Some of the relationships developed in school need to be permanent....When students know that they will spend several years within the same cooperative base group students know that they have to find ways to motivate and encourage their group mates.
>
> Teacher relationships can also be permanent. If teachers followed students through the grades, continuity in learning and caring could be maintained. Better to be taught ninth grade English by a seventh-grade English teacher who knows and cares for the students than by an excellent ninth-grade English teacher who does not know and or care about the students. (pp. 24-26)

When teachers on a seventh grade interdisciplinary team at Tolland Middle School in Tolland, Connecticut, requested to remain with their students in the eighth grade, it initiated a practice that soon spread (Lincoln, 1999). Before the pilot team began the teachers visited other schools, studied the literature, queried parents, and held informal meetings. A formal proposal was presented to the board of education and was approved with the provision that an evaluation be conducted to determine the effectiveness of looping. That evaluation was completely positive with obvious improvements in discipline, attendance, and reduced failures cited. As a result all 18 seventh and eighth grade teachers joined in looping.

The advantages growing out of knowing students better and being able to work on long-term educational objectives, rather than those short-term goals of specific content coverage that seem to dominate the teaching-learning process in most classrooms, were soon apparent to all the Tolland teachers. Parents, likewise, were most supportive. An unsolicited letter (Figure 1) received from parents of a looped student touches on many of the advantages of this long-term teacher-student relationship, and it bears quoting in full here. Especially interesting is mention of the use of the summer between grades for learning experiences.

FIGURE 1

Dr. Robert Lincoln, Principal
Tolland Middle School
Tolland, CT 06084

Dear Dr. Lincoln:

As our youngest child nears the end of his journey at Tolland Middle School, we feel we must comment on the excellent educational preparation our children have received at TMS. The dedicated teachers as well as the many enrichment opportunities afforded our children have prepared them well for the challenges they face at the high school level. We have been particularly pleased with the implementation of looping.

Looping began with our daughter's class, three years ago. When school administrators first broached the subject, we were thrilled with the concept as she was with such a dynamic team of teachers. During the summer between our daughter's seventh and eighth grade, group projects were assigned according to student interests, and our daughter's led to a CT History Day entry. Her group went on trips, worked together in libraries, and basically had a good time while learning. Students came back to school in September ready to present their projects and to begin right where they left off in the classroom. There was no "down time" as teachers and students learned about each other; they were ready to get right to work.

As our son and youngest child was approaching seventh grade, for the first time ever we made a placement request. We so strongly believed in the team my daughter had and the benefits of looping, we requested he too be placed with the same team. With only six months left of his looping experience, both our son and ourselves couldn't be happier with our choice. This age of changes, moods, and ever raging hormones is challenging at best, and often difficult. How fortunate we are to have teachers who really know and understand our son, who can bring out the best in him and overlook the teenage angst. Instead of being with eighth grade teachers who are struggling to understand my son as they begin to teach him, he is with teachers who can guide him, keep him on track, and prepare him for the coming transition to high school by suggesting appropriately leveled courses. His seventh to eighth grade summer project involved our whole family at some point, and led to an incredible expo put on by his team, "Water Water Everywhere." An expo of this magnitude could never be possible without looping. The exhibits demonstrated by this team rivaled anything we'd seen at the high school level.

Our daughter, a product of the first looping team, is a sophomore at Tolland High. She had an easy adjustment to high school and has particularly enjoyed block scheduling. She is consistently in honors and college prep courses, and has been on the honor roll every semester. We feel that the exceptional education she received from her looping team at TMS has been a major factor in her high school success. We look forward to similar successes with our son's high school career, knowing he comes with the best background possible.

We are forever grateful for all Tolland Middle School has given our children. Our only regret is we have no children left to send you. We wish you continued success in the future.

Sincerely, Amelia and Stephen Gudernatch

In the direct and simple way that characterizes most student comments, Justin and Jan, two students at Tolland Middle School, combined their thoughts about the experience they had there.

Last year seventh and eighth grade were looped. It was a good year for everybody who did looping. The students and the teachers have enjoyed it very much.

The reason why we like the looping is because we don't have to play the "name game" at the beginning of the year.

If the teachers are great then you get them again and it's really fun and cool. Instead of taking about 1/2 of a quarter to get to know your teachers and get settled into your new schedule with new teachers, you just get right down to business, and get right down to learning. You also make a lot more friends than you did other years because you know everybody and you can build on the friendships you already had.

Also, the teachers know you better. The teachers all know your learning strengths and weaknesses. So they know how you learn and what kind of extra help you need. All the teachers in my team, Team Blue, have been saying all the report card grades have been higher, also all the tests and quizzes. Most of the homework has been getting in on time, too.

A teacher who is also a parent responded to an inquiry about looping posted on the Middle-L listserve with these off-the-cuff comments:

…actually we do not loop at the school I teach at, however, my own kids are involved in looping. Personally I like it, I think the teachers have a better handle on the kids and I think the summer is much more productive between grades. My daughter went back to eighth grade knowing what would be going on.

Parents worry if they get stuck with a "bad" teacher or if there is a personality conflict …. Personally I think those are excuses…. I think looping is a motivation for working things out, knowing you'll have the student (and the parent) for two years…

I've also heard the argument that they need to get used to lots of people, and they'll have trouble in high school. I don't think there is any evidence to prove that. I am not sure why we are so bent on kids dealing with bunches of people… all with different expectations. Seems to me at this stage they need some order and continuity.

One bottom line, if the teachers aren't on board…looping won't be a positive experience …. But that pretty much is the case with anything.

My son starts the looping process in September, I am very glad. (June 1, 1998)

Teacher-initiated and teacher-developed, the Delta Project (Pate et al., 1993) began as a seed in the minds of two middle school teachers. It quickly grew into a three-year, teacher-student progression or looping project in which four middle school teachers and approximately 100 students (from among roughly 300 students) from Elbert County Middle School in a small rural community in North Georgia, worked and moved together through the sixth, seventh, and eighth grades. A team of university professors collaborated with the teachers throughout the project. The professors acted as a sounding board and as resource persons.

The Delta Project grew out of the concern of a group of middle school teachers for the social, emotional, and cognitive development of their students. These teachers believed that meeting students' social and emotional needs was a necessary prerequisite to addressing their cognitive or learning needs; the teachers believed that addressing the social and emotional needs of their students would help students develop the self-confidence and self-esteem needed for success as a middle school student. Furthermore, they believed that by moving with their students through the middle school years they could more effectively address the social, emotional, and academic needs of their students.

Within the looping structure, the Delta teachers worked to design a program to benefit their students in many areas of their development (cognitive, social, and emotional). To help students maintain an identity within the team, each year teachers assigned students to "base groups." These heterogeneous groups sat together at a table and often worked together on projects. The team was also divided into two sections, so sometimes two teachers could work with half the team on, for instance, science and math, while the other teachers would work in language arts and social studies, and later they would exchange. They implemented a variety of changes in curriculum, instruction, and team organization. The teachers structured their instruction and curriculum to challenge students to use higher-order thinking skills, integrate different areas of the curriculum, and provide students with hands-on, life-related learning experiences. Additionally, their organization for instruction included extensive use of cooperative learning groups that often changed from project to project, and flexible scheduling of instructional time.

It is important to note that the students involved in the Delta Project were assigned to the team through stratified random sampling so that the Delta team was representative in terms of ethnicity, gender, and achievement level of the larger body of students who entered sixth grade at Elbert County Middle School the year this project began. In other words, students were not selected specially for the project, and parents could not petition to have their children assigned to the project. Specifically, the team was composed of 46 males and 54 females; 39 African Americans and 61 Caucasians. They were varied in their levels of socioeconomic status and their levels of achievement.

It was possible for parents and/or students to elect to leave the project at the end of a school year, but this happened only twice (Mizelle, 2000). In both cases, the students were twins. In one case, a girl wanted to be with her twin; in the other case, a twin was moved away from his twin. New students did enter the team as they moved into the school district, but they were not included in the study of the Delta Project; only students who were a part of the project from the beginning to sixth grade were included in the research that was conducted on the project.

A major component of the Delta Project was student collaboration. Students often worked on daily activities and on long-term projects in their base groups. They also completed projects in self-selected or teacher-assigned working groups. Teachers tried to identify activities in which students were actively involved and which were related to their lives. Students were positive about the degree of involvement they experienced. One student said, "Well, there's a whole lot of learning going on. I mean in an interesting way, and the teachers have made learning interesting for us, and I really like it ... you know like not first sitting us down and giving us a workbook" (Pate et al., 1993, p. 26).

Some units were teacher-planned and focused on issues like the environment. Others focused on specific content and still others on themes. Some units involved two teachers, others all four. Many units were developed jointly by students and teachers. Throughout, however, the concept of "one big family" was made operational.

One other noteworthy example of innovation in this area was found at the Manatee Education Center in Naples, Florida, in the early 1990s. Santo Pino, a creative and imaginative school leader and committed middle level educator, had the opportunity to serve as the first leader of a new middle school and a new elementary school, simultaneously and side-by-side on the same campus. Pino organized the elementary school so that teachers and students looped in grades 1-2, and 3-4; not a rare practice. But, uniquely, he also provided for looping to occur from the fifth grade in the elementary school through the sixth grade in the middle school. Fifth grade teachers would move to the middle school with their students; while sixth grade teachers would loop back down to the elementary school to begin a two-year commitment to a new team of students. Then, students would finish the middle school with looping in grades seven to eight. As one might hope, transition problems between elementary and middle school were completely eliminated. If the day ever comes when teams in Naples, and elsewhere, begin looping between the middle school and the ninth grade at the high school, it should have an incredibly positive impact on the success of students during their first year of high school and beyond.

3. SCHOOLS-WITHIN-A-SCHOOL

The schools-within-a-school approach usually retains the basic format of grade level teams, but adds a significant and increasingly popular organizational modification. In this approach, the larger school is divided into houses, villages, communities, neighborhoods, or sub-schools that are representative of the larger school. This organizational arrangement has been operational in many school districts for decades. Recently, it has experienced something of a renaissance as schools have tried to offset increasingly large enroll-ments. The influential Carnegie Corporation report, *Turning Points* (1989), recommended

> The student should, upon entering middle grade school, join a small community in which people – students and adults – get to know each other well to create a climate for intellectual development. Students should feel that they are part of a community of shared educational purpose. (p. 37)

And to create smaller learning environments the report states, "one successful solution to unacceptably large middle schools is the school-within-school or house arrangement" (p. 38).

The burgeoning population in Gwinnett County, Georgia, outside of Atlanta, has put tremendous pressure on its schools. When it opened in August, 1996, Creekland Middle School en-rolled over 2,330 students with about 120 instructional rooms in 276,000 square feet of space. In the fall of 1999 its enrollment had risen to 3,090, making it one of the largest middle schools in the country. An impossible situation? Yes, if the schools-within-a-school concept had not been integral to the design of the school from the beginning. A study team composed of parents, teachers, and administrators reviewed the research data and recommended that the new middle school be organized so that size would enhance, rather than impede, student achievement. The building thus accommodates five "communities," each a microcosm of the total six to eight student body and under the direction of an assistant principal. Even with the ubiquitous portables on site the last two years, the communities remain effective entities for presenting the curriculum in a comfortable climate where students have a sense of identity. The principal, Joan Akin (personal communication, February 14, 2000), a veteran middle school administrator, has always believed that personalized learning should be a priority and asserts that

> The community concept allows Creekland to offer a small school instructional environment while having the advantages of a wide array of co-curricular activities available from the expertise of a large staff.

Personalized learning is achieved by having instructional teams of two teachers with class sizes averaging 26. Teachers share instructional ideas and support as well as sponsorships of activities that invite all students to identify an area of special interest. This helps students "belong" to an organized group while building their own identity.

Parental and student support for the way Creekland is organized is all but universal. Three eighth graders there, when queried on the school-within-a-school concept, were very positive. Ryan said

> I think it is better because you can stay in the same classrooms with the same kids most of the time, but you still have the opportunity to interact with friends from other communities. You see them during exploratory plus after school, but you get to stay with your school friends and make long-term friends in your community.

Aaron added, "I don't think you would have the same relationship in one big school; you would just be acquaintances, not really good friends." Tasha believed, "You get taught better because you have a longer one-on-one relationship with teachers."

One result of the long-term relationship possible in the school-within-a-school was illustrated by Aaron's account of a sixth grade teacher he had two years ago:

> I always liked him as a teacher. We kind of hit it off. He would come to some of my games (when Aaron was a seventh and eighth grader) and I would come back to his room during bus calls and we talk about different things. If I have any trouble, I can fall back on him.

The story of another Georgia school district's plans for new middle school facilities is likely to be repeated many times in the years ahead. Faced with two middle school buildings – both former high schools built in the 1950s – that were beyond being brought up to standard, the Baldwin County Board of Education (located in Milledgeville) opted to build a single facility but accepted the recommendation to design the complex to accommodate four schools-within-a-school. A task force of local educators, parents, and business representatives appointed by the superintendent and board began work in the summer of 1997, more than three years before the building was to be occupied. Working with the architect and the superintendent, the task force approved an initial design.

The plan called for a central level that would contain the administrative suite, technology labs, music, art, and physical education facilities, dining room, media center, theater, and other specialized facilities that would serve the entire complex. Adjoining would be two schools one flight up and two schools one flight down. These identical rectangular-shaped schools will each house just under 400 randomly selected sixth, seventh, and eighth graders. They will be served by a faculty responsible for the academic, special education, and gifted programs. Each school will have its own principal, counselor, and needed support staff. To give the schools an individual identity while not making them competitive and to provide an opportunistic curriculum focus, each school will focus on one of the four regions of Georgia: Mystic Mountains, Historic Piedmont, Coastal Plains, and Golden Isles/Atlantic Coast.

To further provide for long-term relationships and achieve a climate of smallness, students will stay in their particular school for all three years, meet daily with an advisory group of approximately 15 students guided by a faculty member, and have their academic instruction provided by teams of two or three teachers who have ample common planning time.

While students will spend the bulk of the day in their respective houses, they will eat lunch by grade level and participate in exploratories without reference to house. Intramurals and other activities will also mix students from the four schools. Marion Payne (personal communication, March 10, 2000), the Director of Oak Hill, speaks enthusiastically about the potential of this large facility that has been designed to ensure smallness:

> The impact of the decision to build such a facility will be realized well into the future. The paradigm shift that occurred had a very positive effect on the entire community. Numerous hours of preparation in team building activities, program development, staff development, and managing the change process helped to pave the way for the creation of a significantly different and positive school climate. More schools will organize schools-within-a-school. The benefits on student achievement alone will bring this about.

These two recent examples in one state should not mask the fact that there have been dozens and dozens of middle schools operating successfully with variations of the schools-within-a-school organizational plan for decades. One such school is Wakulla Middle School near Crawfordville, Florida, which this year is celebrating its 20th year so organized. The student population of almost 752 students in grades six to eight is organized into three houses: North, South, and East. The hallmark of the process at Wakulla is that each house contains an interdisciplinary team from each grade level, rather than organizing the school by subject departments, as in the traditional junior high school, or by grade level teams as in the conventional middle school. North House, for example, contains a team of teachers and students in each of the sixth, seventh, and eighth grades. Students spend three years in one house, but not with just one set of teachers.

This simple alteration of the physical placement of teachers has had a substantial effect on the culture of the school over the 20 years and leveraged the resulting popularity of the program in the district and the state. The movement of students around the school is dramatically reduced by this arrangement, as students spend almost all of their day in one set of team classrooms next door to one another or across the hall, and almost all of their three years in one wing of the building with lockers and restrooms nearby. The hall becomes a safe haven. The placement of teams in houses, as it was done at Wakulla, meant that incoming sixth graders were dispersed to three houses, and quickly learned not only who their teachers were for the current year, but also who they would be for the next year and the next.

There are many advantages to the schools-within-a-school approach, as implemented at Wakulla Middle School and elsewhere. Students know, from the beginning of their time at the school who their teachers will be for the next three years, and the teachers, likewise, can accurately forecast who will be in their classes one or two years hence. For example, members of eighth grade teams in each house (students and teachers alike) regularly inquire about members of seventh and sixth grade teams from their peers on those teams. Sixth grade students care what eighth grade teachers, in their house, have to say about behavior in the hallways. Eighth grade students care what their former sixth grade teachers think of them. Seventh graders have to look both ways on everything. It is a three-year positive structure without either the intensity or the complexity of multiage grouping or looping. The schools-within-school model may lack the power of the three-year intensity of multiage grouping, but the staff argues that the process is so workable that they have been able to maintain the structure for 20 years at Wakulla with virtually none of the effort that might be required for multiage grouping or looping.

A school publication at pioneering Brookhaven Middle School, in Decatur, Alabama, referred to the concern for the students' sense of identity which resulted when, decades ago, the school was designed in a way that allowed the student to relate to a relatively small component of the total school. At Brookhaven, the staff believed that students' sense of security is fostered, and a spirit of loyalty and pride is developed in a situation small enough for middle school students. As one eighth grader at Brookhaven said, "I feel more loyal to Winter House than I am to the school."

Understanding the developmental level of most middle schoolers, this can be understood as a very positive statement. We now know that student loyalty to larger institutions such as total schools may result from a prior sense of belonging located in the smaller "house." School loyalty, the concern of many teachers and administrators, is not compromised by loyalty to the smaller group; it is enhanced.

Farnsworth Middle School in Guilderland, New York, is in its third decade of excellence with the schools-within-a-school approach. The school's leaders believe there has been "an attempt at harmonizing the best of both worlds – one of which is small enough to foster a leveling of concern for the individual student, and one that is large enough to offer the varied resources necessary to meet the needs and interests of preadolescent and early adolescent youngsters."

The staff at Nock Middle School, Newburyport, Massachusetts, has long supported the idea of having a school-within-a-school, and the students have come to understand its benefits. Nearly 15 years ago, in *Middle Unmuddle*, the student handbook, students explained their understanding of the concept.

HOUSE, SWEET HOUSE

Our Middle School is divided into thirds. These divisions are referred to as the Red, White, and Blue Houses. Each house is to some degree a "school-within-a-school" and every effort has been made to give each house an identity so that we students don't get "lost" in such a large school. The head of each house is the House Coordinator who is, in effect, the "principal" of a school-within-a-school. In each house there are four teams of teachers. Each team of teachers works together to teach us all of our subjects. Sometimes we may have only one teacher in a class; at other times there may be several. Each of us is assigned to a certain house, and within that house we are assigned to a certain team of teachers. Our basic subjects (language arts, social studies, science, and math) will be taught in a block of modes and then there will be other modes set aside for special subjects. This includes art, music, guidance, skill centers, and the SPARK block. The team to which we are assigned will decide what our schedule will be for each day during the basic block.

The schools-within-a-school approach also attempts to assist in the process of articulation on a K-12 basis. This arrangement permits students to enter Nock Middle School from an elementary school and, depending upon developmental maturity, experience a range of options from self-contained classrooms to grade level teams. In the ensuing years, within the same house, students move smoothly and steadily to a more advanced interdisciplinary milieu which will help to prepare them for the first years of high school. Having students spend their entire middle school experience in the same house permits the house faculty to design each student's learning experience much more personally.

At Stroudsburg Middle School in Stroudsburg, Pennsylvania, 1,200 students were divided into two smaller houses, with 600 students in each. Both Mountain and Lake Houses contained students in grades five through eight, and while attempts are made to develop the separate identities of each house, grade level associations were also clearly maintained. This was done not only by locating each grade separately within each house, but by arranging the schedule so that, for example, eighth graders from both houses have the same basic schedule. Eighth graders appeared on adjoining pages in the school memory book, arranged separately by house.

At Nock Middle School, the house identity received slightly more emphasis. Again, 1,200 students in grades five through eight were divided into smaller units, three houses (Red, White, and Blue) of approximately 400 students each. Each house had its own educational leader, team coordinator or house director who, while a master teacher, also assisted in the guidance function. Each house was encouraged to develop a feeling of uniqueness, and the design of the school (with specially colored carpeting for each house, for example) invited this feeling. Oaklea Middle School in Junction City, Oregon, operated in much the same ways, identifying its houses by naming each of them each after a prominent river in Oregon.

Oak Park and Brookhaven Middle Schools, both in Decatur, Alabama, had a long commitment to the schools-within-a-school approach. There, too, each of the three houses of both schools was appropriately named and color-coded to assist in developing the sense of a house or sub-school. Brookhaven chose the names Fall, Winter, and Spring for its houses. Each house had its own student council, and since each house had its own counselor, students developed a three-year long relationship with that professional. Brookhaven staff have been particularly pleased with the cross-age groupings that can evolve from this design.

At Jamesville-Dewitt Middle School in Jamesville, New York, approximately 625 students were arranged into three houses (each including grades five, six, seven and eight). There were four grade level teams per house. Each house had twelve class-rooms, a guidance suite, and a team conference room. The students were randomly assigned to each house and heteroge-neously grouped on each grade level team. Each house had a complement of academic teachers, foreign language teachers, a counselor, and a secretary also serving the students of the house. At Jamesville-Dewitt Middle School the counselor also served as the house educational leader, not so much as an administrator, but reflecting the school's child-centered philosophy, as counselor to the students, consultant to the house teachers, and coordinator and liaison between the house and other adults in and out of the school.

Farnsworth Middle School named its three houses Hiawatha, Mohawk, and Tawasentha after Indian tribes that once inhabited the general area, thus achieving a measure of identity, vicarious distinction, and pride for its students. In this large school (1,650 students in grades five, six, seven and eight) each of the three houses contained approximately 550 students in four or five inter-disciplinary team organizations of 110 to 115 students per team. While separate house identities were encouraged, every team and house was connected both physically and programmatically to the rest of the school. Houses were formed by random assignment of students, but within each house both homogeneous and heteroge-neous ability groups were found. At Farnsworth, each house was directed by its own principal/teacher, and in addition to the regular team teachers, each house had its own secretary, counselor, reading teacher, foreign language teachers, and "learning workshop teacher."

As an illustration of the way in which this arrangement assists in articulation, the fifth grades in each house at Farnsworth Middle School were relatively self-contained. The house principal and the fifth-grade teachers provided the close attention and counseling that they believed the fifth graders required. The house counselors, then, focused their efforts on the students in the sixth, seventh, and eighth grades, and assisted the teachers who were working in the fifth grade. Because the students remained in the same mini-school setting for the four years, the interpersonal knowledge required for a truly supportive interpersonal structure was assured.

Another advantage of having smaller units under the direct supervision of an administrator is the increased ability of that leader to undertake reform and successfully implement improve-ments in curriculum and instruction, to actually become the instructional leader it is widely agreed principals should be. The larger a school the more it resembles a bureaucracy, rather than a community of scholars. In small schools faculties know one another better, have more informal conversations about teaching and learning, and have the security that is needed to take risks and institute changes. The administrator is less burdened with "administrivia" and is more likely to bond not only with the faculty, but with the students.

The long-term relationships established in small schools-within-schools also open the door to the possibility of looping. Teams, having had a successful year, may request to remain with the students a second year. With the endorsement of the parents concerned, such a request can be accommodated. In the same manner, multiage grouping may evolve in such schools.

The Watershed Program

This unique program (Springer, 1994), although it does not match the definition of any of the three organizational arrangements treated in this volume, is, nevertheless, a sterling example of the benefits of a relatively small unit in which students and teachers spend long periods of time together. Mark Springer (personal communication, August 23, 1999), one of the two teachers who directed this special program at Radnor Middle School in Wayne, Pennsylvania, describes the many important benefits of the long-term relationships that occur in Watershed:

> The 36-40 students who elected to be in Watershed each of the last twelve years spent virtually their entire seventh grade year – all day, every day – in a special learning community. While the school's other seventh graders were assigned to large teams with four or more teachers, Watershed students "lived" in one large room and worked with a partnered team of two teachers.
>
> Within this structure our program emphasized caring, cooperation, commitment, and quality as we explored local streams in a truly integrated manner. Our studies involved sharing many experiences from

unusual classroom activities to wonderful excursions into the world beyond the school walls. We hiked our streams and canoed our rivers. We tested the water and met the many creatures who live in the watershed with us. We visited historic, cultural, and important economic sites. We spoke with experts, and we shared our results with the world. We completed many varied community service projects to improve the quality of life in our watershed. And we did it all together, as a small learning community, building trust and mutual respect within a secure yet challenging environment.

The benefits derived from building this type of learning environment seem almost too obvious and too numerous to need delineation. Discipline problems were virtually nonexistent. Indeed, we had a reputation for never sending a student to the school disciplinarian. We didn't have to. The community established its own mutually agreed upon expectations and then supported everyone's attempts to live up to those expectations. The fact that we had all day, instead of a 40-minute class period, meant that we could treat issues in a more global, long-term way. Time did not pressure us into over-reacting in a punitive manner, and we could take the time to look for lasting answers. More important, our time and shared experiences enabled us to get to know our students far better than we ever could in a more traditional school setting. We got to know when and why they were worried, frightened, or upset, and we could act accordingly to prevent potential problems and to assuage their concerns. We got to know why they acted in certain ways, and we got to know how best to treat each individual with respect and caring.

Similarly, we got to know their strengths, their talents, and their weaknesses more thoroughly than teachers can who only see students for 40-some minutes a day. This enabled us to take positive advantage of their assets while also working to help them improve in weaker areas. The consistency of the partnered team structure and the lack of time constraints allowed us to individualize instruction to a greater extent than conventional teaching situations generally allow. This, in turn, helped students improve their skills, particularly in writing and reading.

Tangentially, but no less important, the small learning community structure also gave us as teachers the ability to get to know the parents and families of our students better than we might have otherwise. This added to our abilities to help the students through the increased communication and candor fostered by the deeper parent-teacher relationships.

On a related front, we also witnessed incredible social growth for many of our students. The intentionally heterogeneous nature of our group gave students opportunities to work with students whose talents and strengths might lie in areas other than their own and in other than conventional academic types of intelligence. This fostered increased respect for divergence as it helped academically gifted students see the worthwhile talents and abilities of their less academically oriented peers. Similarly, this structure gave less academically assured students a chance to build their confidence and provide a chance to see and emulate positive role models they would not have seen in a tracked system. Clearly it was – and is – a win-win situation for all students. By year's end, every year, lasting friendships had formed among students of all ability levels and backgrounds – a fact attested to by students who continue to enjoy and enhance those friendships through ensuing years.

Finally, though far from completing the list of benefits, we found the structure of our program enabled our students generally to show more enthusiasm for coming to school each day and about assuming control over their learning. They constantly attribute this positive attitude to the fact that they feel good about their learning community. They take pride in its accomplishments as they feel a genuine sense of belonging and ownership. As one young lady once so admirably said, "Every other year I had a locker; in Watershed I had a home."

Socially, emotionally, and academically, the students truly benefit from the special teacher-student relationships that grow when the time, space, and structure of the educational program intentionally nurture those relationships. So, too, do the teachers benefit. I look forward to going to school each day because I have hundreds of young friends for whom I will always be ready, willing, and able to write letters.

Conclusion

Anyone reading these descriptions and examples of ways to create smallness within bigness by providing long-term teacher-student relationships cannot help but sense the significant educational benefits that ensue. At the same time, it is difficult to see how traditional organizational arrangements could ever achieve these same benefits effectively. As one considers the broad and diverse objectives and goals that schools seek to meet, the advantages that multiage grouping, looping, and schools-within-a-school hold are unmistakable. But is there any research to support these practices? Chapter IV is devoted to that question. ∞

IV
Research on Middle School Organizational Patterns

I n the field of education it is unusual for any particular strategy, method, or program to offer the kind of definitive, hard research data the public and educators themselves would like to have when making decisions. Extraneous factors are almost impossible to isolate when the research subjects are humans. Students bring to school greatly varying prior experiences, and outside of the school day they live in different circumstances. Having said that, the question is still pertinent, is there any research that supports the effectiveness of long-term teacher-student relationship designs? The evidence, while it may be meager and limited in scope, nonetheless does provide considerable support.

There has never been any real question about the proposition that student-teacher relationships are crucial to school success. A caring environment with a teacher or team of teachers inevitably has a positive effect on a child's well-being and attitude about school. And here research does make it clear that students in multiage and looping arrangements evidence clear gains in social and affective skills. According to Darling-Hammond (1998)

> Recent research has found that students experience much greater success in schools structured to create close, sustained relationships among students and teachers. In high-achieving countries like Japan, Germany, Sweden, and Switzerland, teachers often

stay with the same students for two or more years and teach them more than one subject so that their teaching is informed by greater knowledge of the students and how they learn. Studies find that more ambitious learning goals can be tackled with greater success when students' and teachers' work is less fragmented and when the time is available to support serious work.

Teachers are more effective when they know students well, when they understand how their students learn, and when they have enough time with students to accomplish their goals. Studies in the United States have found that small schools and those that personalize instruction by keeping the same teachers with the same students for extended periods of time have fewer behavior problems and higher achievement than very large schools with highly departmentalized structures in which students move continuously from one teacher to another. (p. 20)

Teachers and parents, likewise, benefit from the longer relationships. While on the academic side the evidence is less conclusive, it should be noted, there are no studies that point to any loss in academic achievement. Further, the gains in the affective realm are the ones most likely to provide a positive payoff in life outside of school and in the future.

Early research on school effectiveness

During the 1970s a number of interesting studies identified with the school effectiveness research effort were released. Although looping, multiage grouping, or schools-within-a-school were not specific considerations in these studies, they are relevant for what they demonstrated about the importance of the student-teacher relationship and school climate. After disappointing attempts to revitalize the curriculum and the instructional strategies of newly organized middle schools, educators began to focus on the theme of changing how students and teachers were organized to teach and learn together. This new awareness of the importance of school organization among middle school educators made the research in school effectiveness clearly relevant to the concerns of those educators.

One of the first such studies was conducted by Rutter, Maughan, Mortimore, Ouston, and Smith (1979) in 12 junior high schools in inner-city London. When the study was published, it attracted considerable attention and was discussed in detail in almost all of the reports of research on school effectiveness. It was and is significant for anyone interested in middle level education because of the rigor of the research design and because the findings provided an exciting confirmation of some of the central components of the middle school concept, in spite of the fact that these discoveries occurred in junior high school settings.

The researchers learned that within this sample of 12 junior high schools, several of the schools were very successful while others were not. Successful outcomes were not a matter of grade level or school name, obviously, since all 12 schools had the same name and grade levels. Nor were the successful schools identified by their physical or administrative features, the socioeconomic background of the students, or the differences in the elementary schools that fed the junior highs. The reasons for the success of some of the schools and the failure of others in this study appeared to be outgrowths of two different but closely related sets of factors: academic emphasis and the psychosocial environment.

As had been the case, generally, in the area of research on teacher and school effectiveness, the Rutter study (1979), as it came to be identified, confirmed the importance of an academic emphasis. Reasonably high expectations, direct instruction, homework, and other related items combined to enable teachers and students to take learning seriously and, as a result, to become more successful in mastering the learning tasks. In addition to this academic emphasis, however, the study team concluded that the crucial differences between the successful and unsuccessful schools in the study were the psychosocial environment, that is, the life of the school as a social organization.

65

A positive psychosocial environment was, the authors concluded, the force that permitted teachers to be successful with the academic emphasis in the first place. The academically successful schools were those in which teachers and students saw themselves as part of the same group, as members of the same team. Teachers and students in the schools that reached beyond the expectations or predicted levels of achievement and behavior shared the same educational perspective, the same norms for the life of the school.

Most important, insofar as the middle school is concerned, was that all of the factors that led to the "ethos of caring" characteristic of the successful schools are part and parcel of the American middle school concept. Teachers working together, planning jointly to establish conditions for students, promoting increased responsibilities and participation of students, establishing stable teaching and friendship groups that last for more than one year – all of these factors lay close to the heart of the middle school movement. The Rutter study (1979) understood, and made clear, the insignificance of concerns for the name of the school, the grade levels included, or other factors which have often been mistakenly perceived as important to the middle school by those new or uninformed about the essence of middle level education.

Rutter's team concluded, after four years of study, that the crucial differences in the schools boiled down to whether or not the school effectively attended to the social side of learning. It was critically important, said the report, that teachers and students come to see themselves as part of the same school group, the same team. This unity permitted faculty and students to work together for common purposes in and outside the classroom. Unity is what made it more likely that students shared the educational perspective of the faculty, and what, therefore, led ultimately to higher academic achievement.

Research on multiage grouping

Virtually all of the more recent research studies on school organizational patterns featuring long-term teacher-student relationships have been conducted in the elementary school context with few or no middle or high school examples included. Consequently, there is a great need for data regarding the efficacy of such patterns at the middle school level. Here, we summarize the relevant literature and report in more detail the limited investigations that have focused on middle school organizational patterns.

Three reviews of literature have been conducted on multiage grouping, including Anderson and Pavan (1993), Pavan (1992), and Gutierrez and Slavin (1992). All three reviews focus on multiage grouping at the elementary school.

Anderson and Pavan (1993) conducted a comprehensive review of the literature on multiage grouping as it applied to elementary schools, where nongradedness is used as a synonym for multiage grouping. The authors drew five conclusions:

1. Comparisons of graded and nongraded schools using standardized achievement tests continue to favor nongradedness.

2. Attendance in a nongraded school may improve students' chances for good mental health and positive attitudes toward school.

3. Longitudinal studies indicate that the longer students are in a nongraded program, the more likely it is that they will have positive school attitudes and better academic achievement.

4. A nongraded environment is particularly beneficial for blacks, boys, underachievers, and students of lower socio-economic status in terms of academic achievement and mental health.

5. Further research is needed that includes an assessment of the actual practices in the allegedly graded or nongraded schools in order to determine if the labels as described are accurate. (p. 44)

Pavan (1992) reviewed research conducted between 1968 and 1991 on multiage grouping in elementary schools, comparing student performance using standardized, objective measures of students in a single age group and students in multiage groups. Pavan concluded that comparisons tended to favor multiage grouping. Multiage grouping offered improved chances for good mental health, positive school attitudes, academic accomplishment, and benefits to disadvantaged students.

Both the reviews of research by Anderson and Pavan (1993) and Pavan (1992) look at statistically significant findings favoring single age grading or multiage grading; neither review pays attention to the particular type of multiage grouping used, the methodology of the studies, or the effect of group sizes. Gutierrez and Slavin (1992), however, reviewed research on the achievement effects of multiage grouping by breaking the research into five categories, including (1) nongraded programs involving only one subject, (2) nongraded programs involving multiple subjects, (3) nongraded programs incorporating individualized instruction, (4) individually guided education, and (5) studies lacking an explicit description of the nongraded program.

Gutierrez and Slavin (1992) concluded that positive effects on achievement were found for students grouped in nongraded programs involving only one subject and in nongraded programs involving multiple subjects. Multiage programs that used individualized instruction and individually guided education had less consistent results. Gutierrez and Slavin concluded that multiage grouping can be beneficial to student academic achievement if students are grouped across grades to provide more time for direct instruction.

Beyond the descriptive study by George (1987), a very limited amount of research on multiage grouping has been conducted to date at the middle level. Ashton and Webb (1986) did conduct a study on school organization that involved multiage grouping in middle schools, comparing a traditional junior high school with single-age grouping, departmental organization, and homeroom to a middle school with interdisciplinary teams, multiage grouping, and an advisory program. The purpose of the study was to understand how school organization influenced teacher behavior and thought. Ashton and Webb concluded that the organization of the school promoted different relationships among teachers and led to different views of teaching. Teachers in teams viewed teaching as a communal effort. The authors of the study concluded that the combination of teams, advisory programs, multiage grouping, and clearly articulated goals appeared to lessen teacher self-doubts and increase interdependence.

A study by Nye (1995) concluded that schools implementing multiage structures have not proven detrimental to standardized test scores; rather most multiage-grouped students score as well or better than those in single-grade programs. Student achievement in the area of social or affective domain should favor positive growth. Multiage classroom settings are credited with improving students' attitudes toward school, discipline, attendance, peer relations, and attitude toward work.

Research on looping

Research on the looping model, as such, is sparse. George (1987) conducted a descriptive study at Lincoln Middle School in Gainesville, Florida. A yearlong series of observations, surveys, and interviews conducted in the 1984-85 school year indicated that students, teachers, and parents had positive attitudes toward student-teacher progression and that the degree of positive feelings about student-teacher progression increased as students and teachers remained in the program.

Teachers reported extremely positive feelings about the program. Classroom management was improved, they argued, because of the increased time spent with students. Teachers were able to get to know the students better and became more aware of students' problems both inside and outside of school. Teachers also stated that getting to know students over a long period of time made the advisory role easier.

George (1987) found that discipline was improved by the long-term relationship between teachers and students. He stated, "teachers saw themselves as being much more willing to attempt behavior management alternatives when conventional or accustomed techniques failed to achieve the necessary results" (p. 10). Teachers involved in long-term relationships with students were less likely to use formalized discipline structures, and they were more likely to match a control strategy and alternatives with an individual student's needs.

Teachers believed that their classes developed a sense of community that allowed instructors to ask more of their students. Faculty members reported, additionally, that long-term relationships caused them to be more dedicated and spend more time on their teaching (George, 1987). Teachers stated, furthermore, that long-term relationships emerging from looping allowed more positive relationships to be forged with parents. The faculty reported that they were better able to diagnose student learning needs but required less time for that diagnosis, allowing more time innovative teaching strategies.

Students at Lincoln also had positive views of student-teacher progression. They viewed their teachers as more caring, trusting, and patient (George, 1987). Students felt their teachers believed in them, and the longer students remained in the student-teacher progression program, the more they felt pride in their academic team. Students were more friendly, self-confident, and able to establish friendships with students of other races and backgrounds. Both parents and school administrators at Lincoln Middle School agreed that students benefitted from the increased caring and communication in the student-teacher progression program.

The Attleboro, Massachusetts, school district implemented a student-teacher progression pilot program. The district conducted a survey on the multiyear pilot group and found positive results (Hanson, 1995). Teachers reported that students were less anxious about starting a new school year. The beginning of the second year operated smoothly because both teacher and students knew the expectations. During the second year of implementation, parents reported students had positive attitudes about returning to school. Teachers reported that almost a month of teaching time was gained through the multiyear program, because time spent getting to know their students and time spent on review were not necessary the second year. Learning in the second year could begin almost immediately, and experiences from the first year could be built on during the second year.

Teachers in Attleboro reported that time spent on developing social skills and conflict resolution during the first year paid off the second year. Students who learned to participate in cooperative groups the first year carried that skill over to the second year. Students were better able to resolve conflict and work in-depth with team members. Parents generally supported the multiyear program. Parents liked the idea of becoming comfortable with their children's teachers and with the teachers' expectations. During the second year parents reported feeling more comfortable at parent-teacher conferences.

Teachers in Attleboro also had some concerns about multiyear teaching. Teachers wondered whether a particular makeup of a class could adversely affect the general learning and suggested breaking up such classes. Teachers also warned that special attention needed to be given to students who entered a multiyear class midway through the cycle. Teachers expressed anxieties over their teaching performance being judged over a two-year period on the basis of standardized tests, and felt an intense responsibility for student learning. At the end of a cycle, teachers reported being sad at having to separate from their students (Hanson, 1995).

Tolland Middle School, cited in Chapter III, had all 400 of the seventh and eighth graders participate in looping. In addition to strong support of the parents, a reduction in behavioral infractions, and evidences of the other purported benefits, academic gains were achieved (Lincoln, 1999). Comparative analyses of students' academic grades at Tolland favored the looped group. Eighth grade students earned significantly better grades in language arts than those in the non-looped group. Results of the statewide Connecticut Mastery Test in writing showed statistically significant differences favoring the looped group in eighth grade.

In the first year when both interdisciplinary teams remained together for eighth grade, Tolland students scored eighth best in the state in writing and 15th (of 163 towns/regional districts) in aggregate scores in reading, writing, and mathematics. The same group of students also showed significantly improved scores compared to what they had attained in sixth grade. The percentage of students achieving mastery improved from 41 percent in sixth grade to 79 percent in eighth grade for writing and from 64 percent in sixth grade to 79 percent in eighth grade in mathematics. Looping, it would appear, is a factor in the significantly improved academic performance students showed by eighth grade as measured on these standardized tests. When comparing grade eight, 1996, student writing test (CMT) scores, those of the looped students were statistically significantly better than non-looped students.

A follow-up study on ninth graders provided further evidence. Attitudes of Tolland High School freshmen from looped and non-looped groups were compared in four dimensions: academic competence, social skills, self-efficacy, and attitude toward school. The study included a 50-item survey of 48 freshmen students, 22 from looped and 26 from non-looped interdisciplinary, middle school, seventh-eighth grade teams.

Quantitative research analysis was applied to the data. The looped students scored more positively than the non-looped students on each of the dimensions examined. The looped students scored

- 6.8 percent more positive than the non-looped students in the academic competence dimension.

- 4.3 percent more positive than the non-looped students in the social skills dimension (intra- and interpersonal skills)

- 5.9 percent more positive than the non-looped students in the self-efficacy dimension.

- 15.1 percent more positively than the non-looped students in the attitude toward school dimension (cited by Lincoln, 1999, p. 28).

Burke (1997) reported the results of Project F.A.S.T., conducted in East Cleveland, Ohio, where multiyear teacher-student assignments were a primary component of this pilot project:

Students in the program exhibited substantially higher reading and mathematics achievement scores on standardized tests than did students in the traditional grade organization, even when both groups were taught by the same teacher. In addition to student academic gains, F.A.S.T. teachers reported an increased sense of ownership for student outcomes (both positive and negative), and a heightened sense of efficacy as a result of their increased decision-making autonomy for students. Parents reported feeling more respected by teachers, having more confidence in their children's teachers and administrators, and being more likely to seek the school's assistance with their children.

At Conyers Middle School in Conyers, Georgia, a "progression team" operated over the three-year period 1996-1999. The 53 students that were on the three-teacher team of Carol Brown, Carol Buhler, and Vickie Morrison (2000) all three years included both gifted and special education students. At the end of the third year and the eighth grade, test data favored the progression team who had been "together for every step." The progression team's academic growth on the ITBS was 3.38 years, while for the other eighth graders it was 2.95 years. The progression team's core total ITBS grade equivalent in eighth grade was 10.03, while for other eighth graders it was 8.71.

In addition, student surveys at the end of the eighth grade found 88 percent recommending a future progression team with 79 percent believing their adjustment to middle school was eased by being on such a team, and 85 percent experiencing a grade improvement or stability over three years. Sixty-eight percent of the parents recommended future progression teams for Conyers Middle School. Polling of both students and parents indicates a successful adjustment to high school in 1999-2000, both academically and socially. Weighted GPAs were procured for the 51 students still enrolled in Rockdale County high schools as ninth graders. On a 4.0 scale former progression team members had a median GPA of 3.167.

Research findings on the Delta Project

The Delta Project, a three-year teacher-progression plan, was described in Chapter III. One significant feature of this project was the involvement of three university professors from the project's inception all the way through a high school follow-up component. They documented the changes made by the teachers and the impact of these changes on the students. Data were gathered from questionnaires, permanent records, and extensive interviews with individual students. The research was partially funded through the Eisenhower Act for the Improvement of Mathematics and Science Education, under the Higher Education Section of PL 1002297, Title II.

At the end of eighth grade, when students were asked to reflect on their experience in the Delta Project (Mizelle, 1993), they talked about how staying together with the same students for three years helped them get to know students better, become better friends, and learn to work together as a team.

> It helps a lot because if you're mixed in with groups and they're black and white and girls and boys, then you learn to get along with them better. I know that I've become more open-minded about different people that I thought, you know, when I first looked at them and they were black, I'd say well they might be mean. But now I know that you've got to look inside instead of outside. (Susan, eighth grade interview)

> And I'll remember close friends I've gotten because I wouldn't have met a lot of people, you know, that I've gotten real close with. In fact [if] we hadn't had the second and third year because like the first year, you know, you just go by. But I've gotten closer with some people because of being here three years. (Alice, eighth grade interview)

They also talked about the way having the same teachers from year to year helped them get to know the teachers better and helped the teachers to know the students better. The students felt very close to the teachers; they felt that they could talk to them and trust them. They also saw that staying with the same teachers was a good learning experience: at the beginning of seventh and eighth grade the teachers and students knew each other so they were able to get to work immediately.

> It's just a whole lot of fun being able to talk to your teachers and have them for three years – to be friends with them as well as students. (Sarah, eighth grade interview)

> Like, we've been friends with the teachers for three years, but when you're friends with a teacher, when you're friends, you know, and that person becomes your best friend, you can tell them anything or talk to them. (Cindy, eighth grade interview)

> Yeah, and like the teachers, after three years, they know what you can do, and so you can't always slack off or anything because they know you've done good work before. (Phil, eighth grade interview)

In more general terms, the students observed that staying together for three years made middle school seem more like one long year with several spring breaks, rather than like three separate years. They felt that staying together with the same teachers and students helped them make it through the rough times of middle school. Many of the students even described the Delta team as a family, one big family, and felt that the teachers were closer to the students' families as a result of teachers and students staying together for three years.

> We're in middle school and I don't know if this had a lot to do with it with me, but I know that there are people that go through some pretty rough times at home or places like that when they get this age, and I think it kind of helps to have something that you can ...that is constant. (Susan, eighth grade interview)

75

> Well, I think the teachers and the students in our
> pod are closer because we've been together three
> years. And they know a lot about us. They know our
> families, most of them know our families. And it's
> just…it's just different when you know somebody
> better. (Cindy, eighth grade interview)

The follow-up evaluation study of the Delta Project (Mizelle,
2000) was designed, primarily, to examine the cognitive, social, and
emotional experiences of the Delta students as they made the
transition into high school; it sought to examine how the experiences of the Delta students compared to the experiences of non-
Delta students who moved into the same high school from the
same middle school, but were not a part of the Delta team. Students not involved in the Delta Project experienced a more traditional middle school education with new teachers each year. Their
teachers used few cooperative or hands-on activities and made few
attempts to integrate different areas of the curriculum.

What Mizelle (2000) found was that the benefits of the Delta
Project extended into high school in powerful ways. The Delta
students made higher grades in ninth grade and took higher level
mathematics courses during ninth grade than the non-Delta students. The Delta students were more likely to stay in school and to
graduate on time. As juniors and seniors in high school, Delta
students were more involved in school-related activities and were
elected to positions of leadership more often than non-Delta
students.

Importantly, the Delta students also said that the Delta project
helped them make the transition into high school. It helped them
learn.

> I probably think our pod learned the most. I mean if
> you're not showing it grade-wise, I know people had
> to have learned. It doesn't matter if you're showing
> it grade-wise or not, you know, it's in there, you
> know just don't want to put forth the effort. And I
> think that we probably came in the high school
> knowing, just actually understanding a lot of stuff

better. But it doesn't necessarily mean you're going to put forth the effort. But I think they explained it a lot more clear and made sure we knew what we were trying to do before they just said, "Here's the notes. Take the test." (Alicia, ninth grade spring interview)

It helped them in their interactions with others.

[The Delta project] helped us build friendships and those friendships are still around. (Donna, ninth grade fall interview)

[The Delta project] really taught us how to get along together and how life can be. It makes work easier when you get up here because you have friends. (Heather, ninth grade fall interview)

It helped us learn how to talk to people and we know a lot of teachers so we can tell them any-thing. It helps you trust people more. Gives kids confidence. (Michael, ninth grade spring interview)

The Delta project also helped students feel more self-confi-dent in their ability to learn and to interact with others.

[The Delta project] helped in the self-confidence way. (Jack, ninth grade spring interview)

[The Delta project] taught us how to work together and to work through problems." (Lawanda, ninth grade spring interview)

I think maybe like the students from the Delta team, they don't take stuff as hard as the other students. They can sort of try to not worry as much and maybe work through things better than other students. (Nick, ninth grade fall interview)

We are more comfortable with going to somebody and asking them for help. (Sharon, ninth grade spring interview)

A lot of my friends from the Delta team if they
don't understand it they'll try to find somebody
from the Delta team to help them out and I guess
we're just used to working together. I guess it's a lot
easier to get help from somebody in the Delta team.
But like a lot of the students from other pods and
stuff, it's a lot harder for them if they don't understand something to figure it out than it is for people
on the Delta team, for some of them, not all of
them. I guess we're just used to helping each other
out. (Roy, ninth grade fall interview)

And the Delta project helped students broaden their vision of
what the world ought to be like.

Well, for me I still talk to most of my friends, I
guess I have more, I have a lot of black friends,
more than, I don't know if it's more, but just most
of them from the Delta team I still talk to. I mean
the ones that I see I still talk to. I guess a lot of the
students from other pods probably, they're more like
you know "Ooh, she's black. Let's don't talk to her.
He's white, let's don't talk to him." I don't think
with the Delta team it's like that really. (Roy, ninth
grade spring interview)

And even more importantly, when these same students were
seniors and were asked about the Delta Project, they still felt that
the Delta Project helped them – it helped them learn; it helped
them in their interactions with others; it helped them to be more
confident in their ability; it gave them a sense of stability.

I think that it made people want to learn because it
gave them some kind of this image to help one
another. Like if I could help somebody else or
somebody's gonna be there to encourage me if I
need help. I think it made a difference in the lower
learning kids to say, "Hey, I can do this," and
"somebody's there to help me even if they're not
sitting right there." And still today in a lot of our

high school classes we go over there and help somebody out, you know, as long as you're not giving them the answer. And I think it kind of made those people know how to ask for help, where as they might have sat there and struggled, otherwise.

About the influence of the Delta team on me now? Well, I mean, it taught me how to work with others, of course, how to do the team work and stuff, and even though we don't do a whole lot of group in high school it's still important to know how to relate to others and how to get along with others. But, it gave me more confidence when kids are picking on me (laughter), I guess confidence in myself because I realized that I could help other people, maybe with what I was doing.

Well, I don't know personally if I hadn't been in it, if I wouldn't be where I am today, you know, I can't really say that. But I do think that it did help me in like personal skills and you know, relating with other people that are different from me. Maybe not academically, you know, or I don't know. I think it helped me to understand that there's people who I can help that do have the potential to, you know, be what they can be, but they don't maybe know how to use it or whatever. And I think that by working through groups that helped me, personally, just learn how to work with people from different backgrounds, different family backgrounds from me. (Sharon, 12th grade interview)

[The Delta teachers] showed us how to get along with others, and how to have confidence in yourself – to be able to do your part, and the other person do their part, and be able to combine it all together into one big thing.

> I don't have no problem with, you know, with nobody white, nobody Mexican, nobody of another race… One of my best friends is white, you know. It doesn't bother me, not at all. It's just skin color. We're all the same on the inside. (Nick, 12th grade interview)

> Well, when we were in the Delta team, we had the same teachers. You know middle school's a crazy time anyway, but having the same teachers every year, it was like a foundation. We knew who they were. You adjusted to being comfortable with them and it was easier to move through that time because you felt that the teachers actually knew you. They weren't having to get to know you every year. I guess that they were probably a part in making middle school time more smooth – you know, making the adjustment easier through that time. (Susan, 12th grade interview)

When asked how they felt the Delta students might be different because they were a part of the Delta Project, they pointed to students who they felt were more outgoing, others who were more cooperative and helpful, and others who they felt were better students than they might have been if they had not been a part of the Delta Project.

Finally students agreed that their middle school experience had a positive and more powerful influence on them because the teachers and students stayed together, not just one year, but all three years of middle school. For example, Jack – one of the students who was viewed by other students as having really benefitted from the Delta Project – when asked if he thought staying together for three years made a difference, responded

> Yes, Ma'am, because you can't really get to know a person in a year. But, you know, working with them for three years you got to know them where you could like tell them anything. If you had them one year, you know, you'd still be kind of shy or what

not, but once you get to know them you can tell them whatever.

The reader should understand that this statement came from an African American young man who began sixth grade as a very shy and quiet student yet emerged in high school as a friendly, outgoing, and involved student. He had, in fact, just been voted the "best all around" male student in his class.

Summary

Research on school organizational strategies that create long-term teacher-student relationships is relatively recent, somewhat sparse, and focused mainly on elementary (looping, multiage grouping) and high school (house plan, schools-within-a-school). At those levels, however, the evidence indicates that there may be considerable benefits attached to these strategies. At the elementary level, research on looping and multiage grouping documents advantages for students in academic achievement and in areas of social and personal development. In virtually every study, elementary students involved in looping or multiage grouping perform better on all measures than comparable groups involved in traditional grade level groupings. At the high school level, the existing evidence indicates that schools-within-a-school models may offer real benefits associated with making large, comprehensive schools feel small; houses and career academies seem to offer a sense of place, a feeling of continuity, and an academic focus lacking in larger, more amorphous schools.

Research on these organizational strategies, at the middle school level, remains in a beginning state. Anecdotal reports from practitioners experiencing success and descriptive surveys, such as the authors have reported in this book, do indicate, however, that the results of effective implementation of these organizational strategies will likely provide substantial benefits to students, teachers, and parents. There is, the authors believe, no evidence to deter practitioners from implementing these models and ample reasons to encourage experimentation with these practices at the middle school level. In fact, we exhort practitioners to move forward with such programs as we wait for researchers to conduct studies that will confirm the results that appear to be promised. ☜

V
The National Study

During the 1995-1996 school year we contacted every American middle school that was identified as engaging in some form of long-term teacher-student relationships. A total of 63 schools were initially earmarked; subsequently surveys regarding the practice of long-term teacher-student relationships were mailed to the principal of each of 60 schools. Thirty-three completed surveys were returned, a return rate of approximately 55 percent. This study was conducted to identify, on a national level, the extent to which long-term teacher-student relationships were taking place in middle level education, to summarize the organizational patterns of those relationships, and describe the perceptions of those involved. This study was, therefore, exploratory in nature.

Organization of the study

A concerted effort was made to identify the universe of middle schools that had implemented a version of long-term teacher-student relationships. Officials in each state department of education were asked to identify such schools. The literature was surveyed; professors of middle level education and independent consultants were asked to identify schools for the study. Authors' queries were placed in two professional journals. As a result, 60 schools were identified as appropriate subjects, and surveys for teachers, students, and parents were sent to each of the schools.

Usable responses were received from the following states: Arizona, Colorado, Florida, Georgia, Kentucky, Maine, Missouri, Nevada, New Jersey, New York, Oregon, Pennsylvania, Vermont, and Wisconsin.

Organizational structure of multiyear programs

Of the 33 schools that completed the survey, 17 schools reported using multiage grouping and 11 schools reported using the student-teacher progression or looping model. Each school in the study adapted either the multiage model or the student-teacher progression model to meet the needs of their students; no two schools used either practice in exactly the same way. All of the responding schools did, however, organize and operate in a way that maintained some type of long-term teacher-student relationship.

Thirty-three percent of the schools answering the survey were composed of middle class students from the majority culture. Students from 21 percent of the schools were affluent and from the upper middle class. Fifty-four percent of the schools were middle class or upper middle class; while 35 percent of the long-term relationships were established in schools that served poor, at-risk, or diverse populations.

Schools listed various factors that were important when setting up their programs. Most schools took into consideration one or more of the following factors in developing their programs: student needs, including academic and affective development; gifted students; low-performing students; parent involvement; and administrative support. Several schools reported the desire to have students experience success and to build a community that would help students develop a sense of belonging and greater self-esteem. One school reported that a gifted team of seventh, eighth, and ninth graders made good sense to them. Another school reported that it was important to provide an alternative environment for those students not achieving in the current middle school setting. Several schools reported the need for better parent contacts and more parent involvement in their child's education. The support of the superintendent, principal, and school board was reported by many schools as a necessary element in developing a multiyear program. Often, the administration was the motivating factor that led to the development of long-term teacher-student relationships.

In about a third of the schools, the entire population of the school participated in multiyear programs. The other schools ranged from having just one pilot team to 50 percent of the school being involved in long-term relationships. Thirty-three percent of the schools had only pilot teams, while 66 percent had teams involved in long-term relationships that were considered permanent. Most of the schools surveyed used long-term relationships with sixth through eighth graders, although a few excluded sixth or eighth graders while others included ninth graders. Most of the teams stayed together two or three years. Seventy percent of the schools surveyed had programs that had been in existence only for five years or less, but there were some others that had programs operational for as long as 15, 20, and, in one case, 25 years.

Educators' responses to the survey questions

Educators in each school were asked to respond to a 34-item survey. In some schools, the survey was only completed by an administrator; in others, individual teacher responses were also received. Altogether 105 completed educator surveys were received. The survey provided five options when responding to a question – *strongly agree, agree, strongly disagree, disagree,* and *no opinion/not applicable.* The data reported here, however, have been consolidated by combining the two *agree* and the two *disagree* options and ignoring the *no opinion/not applicable.* The percentages, then, do not add up to 100. It should be noted that the *disagree* option is not indicative of a negative judgment, simply that the item was not influential in that regard.

I. Classroom Management

1. *The long-term teacher-student relationships as organized in our school have permitted our teachers to be more effective in managing student behavior.*

    Agree   89%   Disagree   10%

2. *The long-term teacher-student relationships as organized in our school have been instrumental in producing better classroom discipline.*

    Agree   84%   Disagree   13%

II. Advisor/Advisee Program (Advisory Role)

3. *The long-term teacher-student relationships as organized in our school have been instrumental in bringing teachers to a greater point of student advocacy.*

    Agree   86%   Disagree   12%

4. *The long-term teacher-student relationships as organized in our school helped promote the teacher's role as an advisor, a person concerned about a special group of students.*

    Agree   85%   Disagree   12%

III. Group Involvement

5. *The long-term teacher-student relationships as organized in our school were instrumental in developing a sense of teacher and student identification with the team (a sense of unity and group involvement).*

    Agree   90%   Disagree   6%

6. *The long-term teacher-student relationships as organized in our school stimulated a more intense level of teacher commitment to students, providing special help to those who need it.*

    Agree   81%   Disagree   16%

7. *The long-term teacher-student relationships as organized in our school enabled teachers to be more positive with students.*

Agree   74%   Disagree   24%

8. *The long-term teacher-student relationships as organized in our school enabled teachers to act more fairly in administering rules and levying consequences.*

Agree   73%   Disagree   24%

9. *The long-term teacher-student relationships as organized in our school allowed teachers to become aware of students' personal lives in and out of the classroom.*

Agree   95%   Disagree   2%

10. *The long-term teacher-student relationships as organized in our school provided the time needed for teachers to grow in caring more about each individual student as a person.*

Agree   84%   Disagree   15%

11. *The long-term teacher-student relationships as organized in our school provided opportunities for students on a team to get to know each other better.*

Agree   90%   Disagree   3%

12. *The long-term teacher-student relationships as organized in our school made symbols of group identification assume greater prominence in team life.*

Agree   71%   Disagree   22%

IV. Teacher Investment

13. *The long-term teacher-student relationships as organized in our school have been instrumental in permitting teachers to observe continuous progress and accept some responsibility for the progress.*

Agree   90%   Disagree   7%

14. *The long-term teacher-student relationships as organized in our school have been instrumental in helping teachers get students on task each fall and keep students on task much longer each spring.*

Agree   88%   Disagree   8%

15. *The long-term teacher-student relationships as organized in our school have helped to promote teacher persistence in working with problem students.*

Agree   81%   Disagree   18%

V. Individual Perceptions

16. *The long-term teacher-student relationships as organized in our school have been instrumental in helping our teachers develop a heightened sense of individual student differences.*

Agree   87%   Disagree   10%

17. *The long-term teacher-student relationships as organized in our school have been instrumental in helping teachers discover and build on the strengths of individual students.*

Agree   89%   Disagree   11%

18. *The long-term teacher-student relationships as organized in our school sometimes cause the problem of teacher favoritism of some students to be more serious than it would be in conventional situations.*

Agree   37%   Disagree   60%

VI. Diagnosis

19. *The long-term teacher-student relationships as organized in our school have been instrumental in increasing the amount of knowledge about students that teachers use in diagnosing student needs and evaluating instructions.*

Agree   98%   Disagree   2%

20. *The long-term teacher-student relationships as organized in our school have encouraged teachers to contact parents more frequently in problem-solving situations regarding students.*

Agree 74%   Disagree 21%

21. *The long-term teacher-student relationships as organized in our school were instrumental in increasing teacher accuracy in the diagnosis of student needs.*

Agree 90%   Disagree 5%

VII. Instruction

22. *The long-term teacher-student relationships as organized in our school helped enable teachers to increase the level of time on task in class.*

Agree 76%   Disagree 18%

23. *The long-term teacher-student relationships as organized in our school were instrumental in helping teachers avoid unnecessary duplication from previous years.*

Agree 80%   Disagree 16%

24. *The long-term teacher-student relationships as organized in our school required teachers to have a broader sense of and more familiarity with their subject area.*

Agree 65%   Disagree 27%

25. *The long-term teacher-student relationships as organized in our school encourage teachers to attempt more innovative instructional strategies.*

Agree 74%   Disagree 19%

VIII. Achievement

26. The long-term teacher-student relationships as organized in our school were instrumental in increasing academic achievement for less successful students because of the ability of teachers to prescribe and assess for their students' needs.

    Agree 90%   Disagree 4%

27. The long-term teacher-student relationships as organized in our school help teachers form long-range goals for student achievement and design their instruction with these goals in mind.

    Agree 90%   Disagree 7%

28. The long-term teacher-student relationships as organized in our school were instrumental in making teachers feel more responsible for the success and failure of their students.

    Agree 72%   Disagree 18%

IX. Parents

29. The long-term teacher-student relationships as organized in our school were instrumental in having significant and positive effects on teachers' relationships with parents.

    Agree 80%   Disagree 11%

30. The long-term teacher-student relationships as organized in our school were instrumental in producing a higher level of effective teacher-parent communications.

    Agree 78%   Disagree 14%

31. The long-term teacher-student relationships as organized in our school were instrumental in increasing the involvement of parents of less successful students in and with the school.

    Agree 56%   Disagree 34%

X. Teacher-to-Teacher Relationships

32. *The long-term teacher-student relationships as organized in our school were instrumental in promoting teacher loyalty to and identification with the team.*

Agree   85%   Disagree   10%

33. *The long-term teacher-student relationships as organized in our school were instrumental in promoting an increased level of mutual concern and respect among teachers on the team.*

Agree   79%   Disagree   13%

34. *The long-term teacher-student relationships as organized in our school were instrumental in promoting teacher cooperation and sharing across grade levels and subjects.*

Agree   76%   Disagree   14%

Additional comments from teachers

The 105 surveys completed by educators provided space for additional comments. Most educators' comments regarding long-term teacher-student relationships were very positive toward the programs and complemented the survey items. They indicated that, to them, the positives far outweighed the negatives. A common theme throughout the educators' comments was that effective interpersonal relationships between and among team members, both students and teachers, had to be in place for long-term relationships to work constructively.

One educator stated, "Working in a long-term teacher-student relationship situation has been one of the most positive and productive experiences in my teaching career. The most significant factor in this is working with positive and compatible co-workers." Another educator similarly stated, "I believe the success of such a program is determined by the abilities and compatibility of the team members. For me, it has been the most worthwhile experience of my teaching career."

Another teacher stated, "Student-teacher progression makes teaching even more of a joy." Still another stated, "Long-term teacher-student relationships are an extremely positive experience for teachers and students. In addition to the benefits mentioned in this survey, teaching different grade levels each year makes teaching the same content area far more interesting and challenging."

While most of the educators' comments were positive, some expressed concerns about long-term relationships, particularly about personality conflicts between teachers and students. One educator made the following statement, "Teachers have always felt account-able for their students' growth whether it is a one-year or multiyear connection. The multiyear connection is an advantage for a child with problems. For others, I don't see that it makes a difference. If the teacher-student relationship is not positive, a multiyear connec-tion only makes this worse."

With regard to classroom management and long-term teacher-student relationships, a teacher wrote that these organizational strategies failed to address the problem of non-promotion/grade retention, presumably because in multiage grouping students who are retained would be in virtually the same educational environ-ment they had experienced the preceding year. Other teachers, however, have said that because almost everyone returns the next year, in multiage grouping, the stigma attached to non-promotion is considerably lessened.

A veteran teacher stated

> I have been doing this for twenty-five years and I feel that it is definitely better than a single-year seventh and eighth grade program. I have only found a few drawbacks. Those drawbacks include personal-ity conflicts between students and teachers devel-oped the first year. In certain cases if a student fails the subject he may need a different teacher/approach the second year. Severe discipline problems occurring during the first year may need a team change if teachers feel a change in the student cannot be effected the second year. Some students may get too

accustomed to a particular teacher's approach,
although I feel the benefits far exceed this problem.

Teachers wrote about what they perceived as the obvious advantages of these arrangements for low-achieving students but wrote less frequently about the advantages for able learners.

The survey respondents had many recommendations for schools considering implementing long-term teacher-student relationships successfully. Several reported that enlisting parent support and involvement was essential. Most of those surveyed had implemented a pilot program before broadening it, and they recommended this process to others. A common theme among almost all those surveyed was the need for teacher preparation. Teacher involvement in the planning was also listed as important by several. Some suggested that it was necessary to understand the middle school concept and for the philosophy of the school to be child-centered in order for long-term teacher-student relationships to be effective. Taking curriculum issues into account and making sure materials were appropriate for younger and older students were also identified as important in developing multiyear programs. One respondent suggested, "Changes in the teaming process can affect other teams in subsequent years. Look beyond the first year." Collecting assessment data was identified as important, because careful documentation and evaluation are essential in implementing multiyear programs.

Educator survey responses in summary

The assessment of long-term teacher-student relationships among educators responding to this survey was, in short, enormously favorable. All of the 34 items on the educator survey were answered in positive terms, ranging from a low of 56 percent agreement on item 31, to 98 percent agreement on item 19. The vast majority were in the 75 to 90 percent range. Those practicing long-term teacher-student relationships perceived substantial benefits in the following areas: classroom management; knowledge of and involvement with students and their parents; the development of a sense of community among students and teachers; teacher caring for and investment in students; accurate diagnosis of student needs and prescription of instruction based on those needs; and improvement in teacher relationships.

Educators reported that long-term teacher-student relationships provide teachers with increased effectiveness in classroom management and discipline. Teachers perceived they were able to act more fairly in administering rules and levying consequences when long-term relationships are in place, and they could arrive at higher levels of on-task behavior, particularly in the beginning and the end of the school year. Clearly, respondents believed that longer-term relationships with students helped teachers manage student behavior in their classes more effectively.

Long-term relationships with students, respondents agreed, led teachers to greater levels of caring for those students and to an increased willingness to invest more time and effort in the education of those students. Teachers in long-term teacher-student relationships were more concerned about their roles as advisors and came to be greater advocates for their students. Teachers in long-term teacher-student relationships were enabled to care more about each student as a person and to be much more aware of students' personal lives in and out of school. These practitioners disagreed with the contention that long-term teacher-student relationships would cause the problem of teacher favoritism of some students to be more serious, although a little more than a third indicated there could be a problem in this area.

This increased knowledge of and concern for the students led teachers to invest greater increments of time and energy in the students' educational progress. Long-term teacher-student relationships, educators reported, stimulated a more intense level of teacher commitment to students and to providing more special help to students who required it. Teachers developed a greater sense of professional efficacy, perhaps, from being able to observe continuous progress in their students from year to year. The duration and quality of teachers' relationships with students promoted their persistence in working with problem students, in circumstances that might have, without long-term teacher-student relationships, been more discouraging. Respondents related their belief that teachers felt more responsible for the success and failure of their students.

Survey respondents, then, reported that teachers came to know and care more about their students, and that this caring brought them to a greater willingness to invest time and effort in their students' education. Knowledge, caring, and investment, consequently, combined to produce greater accuracy in diagnosing and prescribing for the instructional needs of middle level students. Teachers developed a heightened sense of individual student differences and were able to discover and build on the strengths of individual students. Respondents asserted that this increased effectiveness in assessing and prescribing for students' needs was particularly beneficial when it came to the education of students who had been less successful.

A more accurate diagnosis of student needs led teachers to make more effective plans for instruction. Teachers, for example, were able to avoid unnecessary duplication of lessons from previous years. As a consequence of teaching across the spectrum of their subject area, teachers came to have a broader sense of and greater familiarity with that subject area. Teachers in long-term teacher-student relationships were inclined to attempt more innovative methods and design instruction with long-range achievement goals in mind.

Relationships between teachers and students that last for more than one year tend to create a broader educational community with more intensity and meaning with both students and teachers strongly identified with their team. Students got to know each other better, and symbols of group identification (e.g., team names, banners, logos, colors) assumed more prominence.

Teachers' relationships with parents were reportedly more positive and produced more effective teacher-parent communications. Relationships between and among teachers on teams characterized by long-term teacher-student relationships also reflected the benefits of that greater sense of community, with greater teacher loyalty to and identification with the team, increased mutual concern and respect, and more cooperation and sharing across grade levels and subjects. Clearly, these educators perceived extensive benefits accruing to group involvement and a sense of community as a result of long-term teacher-student relationships.

Student responses

Over 1,100 students responded to a 10-question survey. As in the case of educator responses, the survey provided five options, but they are reported here with the *agrees* and the *disagrees* combined and with the *no opinion* option left out. Some sample student comments are included.

1. *I like staying with the same teachers for more than a year.*

    Agree   71%   Disagree   27%

    I enjoy staying with the same people. I feel closer to everyone.

    I would really recommend this! The only bad part about it is going to be leaving them – they've become so close to me. I'll really miss them.

    I don't like staying with the same teachers because if you get a bad teacher, you have him or her for two years.

    I think if we would go to different teachers we would learn more because teachers are not the same and they know different stuff.

2. *Staying with the same teachers and students for more than one year helped me to get to know other students better.*

    Agree   78%   Disagree   20%

    Staying with the same students for more than one year taught me new strategies because I watched and saw how they dealt with problems and it worked for me as well.

3. *Staying with the same teachers and students for more than one year helped me better understand what my teachers expect of me.*

Agree   82%   Disagree   16%

I liked to move up with my teachers because I knew what to expect.

When you have the same teachers for three years it saves time because the teachers already know you and what you learned last year.

I liked staying with the same teachers for two years because I went to school knowing what the teachers expected of me. I felt more comfortable because I came to school already knowing my teachers.

4. *Staying with the same teachers helped me to get to know my teachers better.*

Agree   84%   Disagree   14%

Having the same teachers for two years in a row really takes the stress out of the beginning of the year because you know if you are getting a good teacher or not.

I enjoyed belonging to Core II as a group. But I would enjoy getting out more to experience different styles of teaching and learning.

I don't like staying with the same teachers because you had nothing to look forward to at the beginning of school. And they (teachers) act like your parents.

I do not like having the same teachers and students for more than one year. I want to be able to be in different classes with different teachers and students, so I can be able to explore and see how different teachers teach their students and see how students react to the teacher's teaching. The teacher may not really like you and then you could be stuck with each other for two years.

I liked staying with the same teachers very much. I like all my teachers but one and think the two-year system works very well.

5. *Staying with the same students for more than one year helped me make more and better friends.*

Agree   72%   Disagree   24%

It's fun to stay in the same group if your friends are in that group.

This has been the best two years of my social life.

I loved being with teachers and friends. I have had the best teachers and my friends are really great that I made on our team in middle school.

6. *Staying with the same students for more than one year helped me be friends with different kinds of kids.*

Agree   64%   Disagree   32%

I strongly believe that teams or groups are great for all kinds of kids.

My Delta team will help many different kinds of kids.

7. *Staying with the same teachers and students for more than one year helped me feel like I really belong to my group or team.*

Agree   64%   Disagree   33%

Staying with the same kids year after year helped me to feel more comfortable about coming to school.

I really like staying with my team. It's my second family.

The Eagle team is a good experience and I feel comfortable around them (the teachers), but I wish sometimes we could hang out with our other friends more than one period.

The last school I went to was very different. Things felt out of place. Here I feel like I belong, like I have a new home.

The team I was on is great! I wish for my brothers to get on this team.

8. *Staying with the same teachers for more than one year helped my teachers know me better and care more about me.*

    Agree   69%   Disagree   26%

    Staying with the same teachers for more than a year helped because the teachers knew me and they knew what type of problems I might have.

    I am not a good student but my teachers know my problems and go out of their way to help me do better.

9. *Staying with the same teachers for more than one year helped my teachers trust me.*

    Agree   71%   Disagree   25%

    I really like my teachers. I hope they can trust me because I can trust them. I am glad I've pretty much been with this group of teachers and friends for three years.

    I don't really think staying with a teacher more than one year helps her/him trust me, or like me.

10. *Caring about my teachers and feeling part of a team has helped me build my self-confidence and feel good about myself.*

    Agree   57%   Disagree   35%

    I think staying in the same core for two years helped me, because I could stand up and tell a speech without being afraid because I already knew everybody for two years.

I have accomplished things because of the support on Delta. I have also gained self-confidence which will help me make my way through life.

This program helped me build confidence, but it was only successful because the teachers were excellent. It was a hard transition to the huge environment of high school because the team was such a protected environment.

Other student comments not related to the 10 questions

They should do this in high school.

I would like to be on a multiage team in high school with the students from my school.

Summary comments on student responses

In general, students were positive about long-term teacher-student relationships but not nearly as positive as their teachers. Students reported that long-term teacher-student relationships contributed to improved relationships with other students. They believed they were able to make more and better friends with different kinds of students and develop a feeling of belonging to the group or team.

Staying connected to the same teachers for more than one year, students reported, also helped them get to know their teachers better. This increased interpersonal knowledge helped teachers know and care more about the student and helped teachers develop greater trust in the student. A slight majority of students believed that caring about teachers and feeling a part of a team resulted in increased self-confidence and self-esteem. While students appear to prefer long-term relationships with teachers and other students, they, not surprisingly, recognized the importance of having good teachers to make it successful.

Parent responses

A total of 586 parents from the 33 schools completed survey forms. As before, the data are summarized by combining the two levels of *agree* and *disagree,* and some sample parent comments are included.

1. *Having my child stay with the same teachers for more than one year has encouraged my coming to the school for visits.*

    Agree   46%   Disagree   40%

    I would come more if I didn't know the teachers.

2. *Staying with the same teachers for more than one year has helped my child to be successful academically.*

    Agree   64%   Disagree   26%

    It depends strictly on the teacher. One, I would love to have each year. Another, I would hope never to have again. It does help however in learning what the teacher expects, her style, grading, etc.

    I think the strong points of long-term teacher-student relationships are: allows continuity of curriculum and should allow students to progress at their optimal individual pace.

    My son had a poor science program for three years. Three years is too long to have the same teachers. Two years may provide benefits to the school, child, and teacher, but three years is too long.

    My child has "blossomed" both academically and socially under this program. I feel it has been a very positive aspect of her middle school development.

    My child has been on the MAT team for two years. The second year of MAT was the smoothest start of the school year that we have ever experienced. There seemed to be much less wasted time spent on reviewing subject matter and getting to know classroom routines.

3. *I would like my other children to have the experience of a long-term relationship with teachers and students.*

Agree   61%   Disagree   21%

The only negative aspect of this system, as it pertains to my child, is that it is harder to leave these teachers at the end of the eighth grade.

4. *This system has helped to make a large school feel small.*

Agree   66%   Disagree   22%

This program has made it possible for the teachers to become aware of Heidi's personal needs. It has made it so she is not just another number at a large school.

I don't feel that staying with the same teachers is beneficial to our children. Teachers form certain expectations that can negatively affect student performance and motivation. Also by making their middle school environment so comfortable and "secure" they are not adequately preparing them for high school. Making the transition from a "small" personal atmosphere to a much larger and impersonal environment will be quite a daunting task for our children.

5. *Staying with the same teachers helped the teachers to know better and accept my child.*

Agree   81%   Disagree   17%

The system has been a wonderful way for the teacher to understand some of the other dynamics of my child and assist him to succeed. I am truly grateful for this wonderful group of professionals.

In my son's case the teachers knew him so well that if something was bothering him or he began to fall in his work they picked up on it. I met with the team quite a few times and it made the meeting easy – they had insight into my son.

This has been a wonderful program for my child and I appreciate all who have taken part in this endeavor. I have seen major growth in self-esteem and leadership in my child since becoming involved in this program two years ago.

My child has ADD and I believe has benefited from having the same teachers who are more aware and sensitive to his problems and are willing to go the extra mile for him.

I like the continuity, the feeling that my child's teachers know her better than if they only had her for a year. However, I want to add that I'm glad she got the team she did or I would not have been a proponent of this system.

6.   *Spending more than one year together is an effective way to organize the school.*

Agree   67%   Disagree   25%

Overall, this system has been very positive for our child. The transition period of going from seventh to eighth grade was eliminated. There was no need for the "getting to know you stage."

As a parent I was very happy and impressed by the six/seven team. What impressed me the most about the teachers was their enthusiasm and that they seemed to genuinely like the children which can be hard given their personalities and behavior at their ages.

7.   *Having a poor teacher for three years has been a serious problem for my child.*

Agree   31%   Disagree   42%

Some teachers are there only for their paycheck. This system doesn't work well if your child has a teacher like that.

Staying with the same teachers for two years is a fine idea if the teachers are excellent. I found it difficult if the teacher is boring or not a very good teacher.

The system is only as good as the teachers are.

Three years is too long – I think the kids are onto the teacher's rules, etc. and take advantage. If a student can't relate to a teacher or turns off in class because of a teacher (no fault of the teacher, just bad chemistry) change might be good.

8. *This system has helped me get to know my child's teacher much better.*

Agree   34%   Disagree   58%

I feel that having the same teacher has been very good. I don't feel that I have to be at the school keeping track of what is going on because in the first two years I learned to really trust the teachers.

9. *Given the opportunity, I would want my child to have all new teachers each year.*

Agree   34%   Disagree   58%

I feel that the students should be exposed to having different teachers each year because students tend to become "too comfortable" with the same teachers. Children should also have new and different students.

My child's teachers made up their minds the first year about what kind of student my child was. The teachers' attitudes did not change for three years and I feel this is harmful to my child. When a child is expected not to perform, the child usually doesn't perform.

My child's experience was good. However, if student/teacher/parent problems existed during the first year, I would not want my child placed with the same team for a second nonproductive year.

10. *My child had difficulty in this system because of personality conflicts with the teachers.*

Agree   22%   Disagree   67%

This system has allowed my child to work around those teachers she had a personality conflict with. This permitted her the opportunity to learn conflict resolution at an early age. I particularly found this method of teaching helpful for the large class size in today's system.

Parent responses not related to the questions

I would like to know that all teachers and students are in on the "Team" process, including Art, Music, P.E., etc.

If middle school is supposed to prepare one for high school having the same teachers is not doing this task!

I can see where it has benefits and negatives. Overall, I like the program and see where it can help most children transition to higher grades (create more responsibility).

Problems

I wish they would do this in high school grades also to better prepare our children for the years beyond the classroom.

We have been very impressed with our daughter's teachers. They all are caring and creative and show an enthusiasm for their subjects which is shared by their students. It's a shame they can't follow the students to high school.

We are very pleased with the MAT team. We are hoping this can be carried on to high school.

This program has been wonderful for my child. She has made many close and hopefully long-lasting friends.

This works well with some students, but not all. Give the student the option to change teachers at the end of the year.

This program took our student out of the mainstream of building social relationships with other kids of her own maturity level. She felt left out and excluded from regular grade level activities.

Parent responses in summary

Parent comments regarding long-term teacher-student relationships, received from 586 respondents, might be characterized as modestly positive – less so than either their children or the educators, but positive nonetheless. More than three-fourths of the parents reported that long-term teacher-student relationships had helped teachers know their child better and accept him/her more readily. A solid majority of parents believed that staying with the same teacher for more than one year had helped their children to be successful academically and reported that they preferred such an arrangement for their other children. While most of the parents reported that personality conflicts with teachers were not a problem for their children, some did agree that having a poor teacher for three years had been a serious problem for their child.

Parents had several other reservations about long-term teacher-student relationships in their school. They split almost equally on the question of whether long-term teacher-student relationships encouraged parents to come to school for visits and whether long-term teacher-student relationships had helped them get to know their children's teachers much better.

A small group of parents (12 out of 586) felt so strongly about their children's experience with long-term teacher-student relationships that they wrote extended comments on the survey forms. In essence, these parents were concerned about two things: having a poor teacher or a team of poor teachers for more than one year, and having their children exposed to fewer teachers and students than would be possible under traditional circumstances. A close reading of their responses indicates that these parents seem to have children who might be described as "high ability, high achieving." Their concerns seemed, in large part, related to their children experiencing less academic challenge and stimulation as a result of the second or third year as a member of a long-term team. Even with these parents, however, fully half of the comments indicated that it was the potential for having a poor teacher, rather than the actuality, that most concerned them; many went so far as to say that their own children had been extremely fortunate to have high-quality teachers.

Generalizations derived from teacher, student, and parent comments

All three groups of respondents seem to agree on several areas. Students, teachers, and parents agreed that long-term relationships helped teachers, students, and parents experience a greater sense of community. The groups also agreed that relationships between individual teachers and students, parents, and other teachers benefited from continuing those arrangements for more than one year, with increasing interpersonal knowledge, caring, trust, and accurate perceptions as outcomes. The qualities of these relationships, furthermore, contributed to improved educational diagnosis and instructional planning. Finally, while the three groups appeared to be apprehensive about the damage that might result from poor human relationships in a long-term teacher-student situation, and about students who might suffer from exposure to poor teachers for more than one year, few actually reported that they had experienced such a situation.

Based on the responses to the three surveys that comprised this investigation, it seems safe to say that the subjective assessment of long-term teacher-student relationships ranges from slightly positive among parents to moderately positive with students, to strongly positive among educators. In each case, negative responses seemed limited to a very small minority of respondents, but those responses might represent intense feelings that, if expressed publicly, would carry greater weight. They should, therefore, be recognized and treated proactively. ∞

VI
Guidelines for
Implementation and Conclusions

School leaders who anticipate the implementation of an organizational arrangement that provides long-term teacher-student relationships and helps to achieve a sense of small-ness should be encouraged by the information and data reported in this publication. Nonetheless, careful planning and comprehensive involvement of teachers, parents, and community members in the development of the program is essential.

The administrative side of the task is the easy part. What takes time, study, discussion, and careful communication are the public relations aspects of implementation. Judgments have to be made about the readiness of the faculty, the parents, and the community to undertake a program. Specific staff development activities must be provided, and curriculum adjustments are needed, but even more important is dealing with attitudinal factors.

Local conditions and circumstances vary widely, so what follows is cast not as a set of recommendations, but rather as a list of factors or guidelines to consider. They reflect the experiences of those participating in the national survey, other practitioners cited, and the cumulative experiences of educators. Most of them apply more to multiage grouping and looping than to the schools-within-a-school design.

1. While in every educational enterprise the truism "the teacher makes the difference" is applicable, in implement-ing multiage or looping arrangements, it is the critical

truth. Unless parents are more than merely satisfied with a teacher or team, they will fight plans to subject their children to a second or third year under such a teacher's or team's tutelage. Clearly, if there is one major generalization that will ensure the success of a long-term teacher-student relationship program, it is having quality teachers.

2. Practices that yield long-term teacher-student relationships, however desirable, are not ones that should be implemented by administrative fiat. Such arrangements are best achieved when the initiative comes from teachers who express a desire to participate in such ventures.

3. It is perhaps wise to start with a pilot team or two before attempting to make long-term teacher-student relationships universal in a school. These pilot teams should have ample planning time and perhaps some other forms of support as they prepare to launch the program. Visiting schools practicing long-term teacher-student relationships, attending conferences, and reading and discussing relevant literature are all valuable activities for those interested.

4. Strong administrative support is essential. It must go beyond a willingness to permit the project to go forward and include a genuine philosophical commitment to the concept and the ability to articulate it to others.

5. Develop a plan for how the project will be assessed before it is launched. Determine what baseline data are available and needed. Select and/or develop instruments by which to determine the effectiveness of the project. It is particularly crucial that data on student achievement be included.

6. Consider possible certification problems and how they might be alleviated via issuing waivers or earning specific course credits.

7. Recognize openly to all involved that implementing long-term teacher-student relationships will require additional time and effort to be successful. Entering into a project should not be done lightly. A commitment from those

directly involved to stay the course for the cycle whether it be two or three years is needed.

8. Expect some resistance from faculty members not involved in the pilot teams, whether their objections are based on jealousy, insecurity, or honest differences in philosophy. The entire faculty needs to be informed and have opportunities to raise questions and receive progress reports as the project moves along.

9. It is probably better to start with a two-year program of looping or multiage grouping that does not include grade eight.

10. The need to inform and involve parents as much as possible cannot be overstated. This includes both discussions well in advance of implementation and periodically during the initial year. Because the project includes a major deviation from traditional practices, parents will be concerned and are likely to be skeptical. Parents of high ability students are most likely to have reservations about the experiment, fearing that their children will not be challenged. The opportunity for parents to opt out should be provided if possible.

11. Students placed on a multiage or looping team should comprise a heterogeneous group. In particular, avoid overloading pilot teams with so-called gifted students.

12. In like manner, when establishing two or more schools-within-a-school, the units should conscientiously be organized so that they are equal or balanced both in terms of students and faculty. This will avoid the many problems that would occur if one unit were seen as the quality or preferred unit.

13 The students involved in any new organization will need to be prepared and have an understanding of the rationale and expectations.

14. The quality of the student-teacher relationship is particularly critical in long-term relationship designs; therefore,

extensive efforts should be made in the first weeks of implementation to develop a strong bond among and between the students and the teachers.

15. A host of curriculum issues need to be dealt with when a multiage or looping project is undertaken. Identifying and discussing these issues will require extensive discussions over time. Where state-mandated tests parallel a graded curriculum, obvious conflicts arise.

16. Administratively providing for long-term teacher-student relationships that will foster a sense of smallness will not, in and of itself, ensure improvements in students' achievement or development. Teachers concerned will need to alter more traditional ways of instructing and take to heart the warning of Henry David Thoreau who said, "Beware of enterprises that require new clothes, but not rather a new wearer of clothes."

17. Uninterrupted blocks of time are essential for multiage grouping and greatly to be preferred in any plan.

18. Multiage classrooms inevitably will bring into play thematic and skill-based instruction as opposed to logical content-coverage, one-lesson-for-all approaches.

19. New, broader means of assessing progress must be developed. Assessment measures tied to grade level standards need to give way to evidences of progress, not only in content acquisition, but in other goal areas.

Conclusion

As American society becomes larger and more complex, so do all of the institutions in which citizens abide and conduct their lives. Government, corporations, health care, the military, and schools too evolve toward a more technological, high-pressure, accountability-based organizational climate. The human scale so necessary for healthy, productive lives seems to recede further and further from the daily experience of everyone involved. If our institutions are to retain the productivity we require, even as they grow in size, they must be reorganized in ways that allow long-term, high quality human relationships to thrive. It appears that the public school is the one major institution in the best position to counter the trend toward impersonal, bureaucratic operations. As typically organized, however, middle and high schools are a part of the problem rather than a part of the solution. Implementing one of the ways to provide a sense of smallness can put schools in the solution category.

Adding the component of long-term teacher-student relationships to those characteristics that have come to be identified as comprising the middle school concept is now in order. Educators in 21st century middle schools can and must rise to the challenge of organizing their schools so teachers, students, parents, and administrators can work together to fashion true learning communities that seem small and are characterized by significant interpersonal relationships. The knowledge and experience required for such organizational transformation to take place is available; only the will needed for more widespread implementation is lacking. For the sake of our all too vulnerable society as well as the education of young adolescents, it must be done. ∞

References

A conversation with...Jim Grant (1998). *Middle Link, 29.*

Advancement of the teacher with the class. (1916). Bulletin 1915, No. 42. Bureau of Education, Department of the Interior.

Anderson, R. H., & Pavan, B. N. (1993). *Nongradedness: Helping it to happen.* Lancaster, PA: Technomic Press.

Arhar, J. (1992). Enhancing students' feelings of school membership: What principals can do. *Schools in the Middle, 1* (3), 12-16.

Arhar, J., & Kromrey, J. (1993, April). *Interdisciplinary teaming in the middle level school: Creating a sense of belonging for at-risk middle level students.* Paper presented at the Annual Meeting of the American Educational Research Association, Atlanta, Georgia.

Ashton, P. T., & Webb, R. B. (1986). *Making a difference: Teachers' sense of efficacy and student achievement.* New York: Longman, Inc.

Beane, J. (1997). *Curriculum integration: Designing the core of democratic education.* New York: Teachers College Press.

Brown, C., Buhler, C., & Morrison, V. (2000, February). Student-teacher progression...together for every step. Presentation at Georgia Middle School Association annual conference, Atlanta, Georgia.

Burke, D. (1997). Looping: Adding time, strengthening relationships. *ERIC Digest.* Eric Document Reproduction Service No. ED 414098.

Carnegie Council on Adolescent Development (1989). *Turning points: Preparing American youth for the 21st century.* New York: Carnegie Corporation of New York.

Darling-Hammond, L. (1998). Alternatives to grade retention. *School Administrator, 55* (7), 18-21.

Flowers, N., Mertens, S., & Mulhall, P. (1999). The impact of teaming: Five research-based outcomes. *Middle School Journal 31* (2), 57-60.

George, P. (1987). *Long-term teacher-student relationships: A middle school case study.* Columbus, OH: National Middle School Association. *school* (2nd ed.). Fort Worth, TX: Harcourt Brace.

George, P., & Shewey, K. (1994). *New evidence for the middle school.* Columbus, OH: National Middle School Association.

Grant, J., Richardson, I., & Forsten, C. (2000). In the loop. AASA School Administrator. Retrieved February 23, 2000 from the World Wide Web: http://www.aasa.org/sa/jan0005.htm.

Guiterrez, R., & Slavin, R. E. (1992). Achievement effects of the nongraded elementary school: A best evidence synthesis. *Review of Educational Research, 62* (4), 333-376.

Hanson, B .J. (1995). Getting to know you: Multiyear teaching. *Educational Leadership, 53* (3), 42-43.

Hirschi, T. (1969). *Causes of delinquency.* Los Angeles: University of California Press.

Homans, G. C. (1950). The human group. In D. Levine and H.D. Lasserwell (Eds.), *The policy sciences* (pp. 44-69). Stanford, CA: Stanford University Press.

Hopping, L. (1999). *Multiage teams – Crabapple Middle School, Roswell, Georgia.* Unpublished manuscript.

Johnson, D., & Johnson, R. (1989). *Leading the cooperative school.* Edina, MN: Interaction Book Co.

Kramer, L. (1990, April). *A comparison of at-risk and successful students' school experiences in a multicultural junior high.* Paper presented at the Annual Meeting of the American Educational Research Association, Boston, MA.

Lincoln, R. (1999). Looping: A matter of time and relationships. *The Journal of the New England League of Middle Schools, Spring, 7-11.*

Lloyd, L. (1999). Multiage classes and high ability students. *Review of Educational Research 69* (2), 187-212.

Lounsbury, J., & Vars, G. (1978). *A curriculum for the middle school years.* New York: Harper & Row.

Lynch, J. (1990). *Evaluation report for Skowhegan Area Middle School.* Skowhegan, ME: School District #54.

Makeshift Cobb school makes grade. (1999, September 25). *Atlanta Journal-Constitution,* pp. E1, E8.

McEwin, C. K., Dickinson, T. S., & Jenkins, D. M. (1996). *America's middle schools: Practices and progress — A 25-year perspective.* Columbus, OH: National Middle School Association.

McLaughlin, H. J., & Doda, N. M. (1997). Teaching with time on your side: Developing long-term relationships with schools. In J. Irvin (Ed.), *What current research says to the middle level practitioner* (pp. 57-71). Columbus, OH: National Middle School Association.

McLaughlin, H. J., Irvin, J. I., & Doda, N. M. (1999). Crossing the grade level gap: Research on multiage grouping. *Middle School Journal 30* (3), 55-58.

Meier, D. (1996). The big benefits of smallness. *Educational Leadership 51* (1). 12-15.

Mizelle, N. B. (1993, April). *Classroom structures and student motivation: A study of the Delta project.* Paper presented at the Annual Meeting of the American Educational Research Association, Atlanta, Georgia. (ERIC Document Reproduction Service No. ED 359247)

Mizelle, N. B. (2000). *The Delta Project.* Unpublished manuscript.

Moskos, T. C. (1975). The American soldier in combat in Vietnam. *Journal of Social Issues,* 25-39.

National Middle School Association (1982). *This we believe.* Columbus, OH: Author.

National Middle School Association (1995). *This we believe: Developmentally responsive middle level schools.* Columbus, OH: Author.

Newmann, F. M. (1981). Reducing student alienation in high schools: Implications of theory. *Harvard Educational Review, 51* (4), 546-564.

Nye, B. (1995). Are multiage/nongraded programs providing students with a quality education? Nashville, TN: Center of Excellence for Research in Basic Skills. (ERIC Document Reproduction Service No. ED 384998)

Ouchi, W. (1981). *Theory z.* New York: Addison-Wesley.

Pate, P., Mizelle, N., Hart, L., Jordan, J., Matthews, R., Matthews, S., Scott, V., & Brantley, V. (1993). The Delta project: A three-year longitudinal study of middle school change. *Middle School Journal, 25* (1), 24-27.

Pavan, B. N. (1992. April). *School effectiveness and nongraded schools.* Paper presented at the annual meeting of the American Educational Research Association, San Francisco.

Peters, T., & Waterman, R. H., Jr. (1982). *In search of excellence.* New York: Harper & Row.

Rohlen, T. P. (1983). *Japanese high schools.* Berkeley, CA: University of California Press.

Rosenholtz, S. J. (1989). *Teachers' workplace.* New York: Longman.

Rutter, M., Maughan, B., Mortimore, P., Ouston, J., with Smith, A. (1979). *Fifteen thousand hours: Secondary schools and their effects on children.* Cambridge, MA: Harvard University Press.

Schmuck, R. A. (1982). *The school organization and classroom interaction once again: School climate.* Paper presented at the 1982 Annual Meeting of the American Educational Research Association, New York.

Slavin, R. E. (Ed.). (1989). *School and classroom organization.* Hillsdale, NJ: Erlbaum.

Smith, C. (1999). *Multiage classrooms.* Unpublished manuscript.

Springer, M. (1994). *Watershed: A successful voyage into integrative learning.* Columbus, OH: National Middle School Association.

Study: Rich, poor school gap increases with size. (1999, December 11). *The Atlanta Journal-Constitution*, p. G3.

Veenman, S. (1995). Cognitive and noncognitive effects of multigrade and multi-age classes: A best-evidence synthesis. *Review of Educational Research, 65* (4), 319-381.

Wehlage, G. G., Rutter, R. A., Smith, G. A., Lesko, N., & Fernandez, R. R. (1989). *Reducing the risk: Schools as communities of support.* Philadelphia: Falmer Press.

Williamson, R., & Johnston, J. H. (1999). Challenging orthodoxy: An emerging agenda for middle level reform. *Middle School Journal, 30* (4), 10-17.